Luke, a Plagiarist?

Luke, a Plagiarist?

George E. Rice

Pacific Press Publishing Association
Mountain View, California
Oshawa, Ontario

All Bible texts in this book are from the Revised Standard Version.

Cover photo by Joan Walter

Copyright © 1983 by
Pacific Press Publishing Association
Printed in United States of America

Library of Congress Cataloging in Publication Data

Rice, George E., 1933—
  Luke, a plagiarist?

  Includes bibliographical references.
  1. Bible. N.T. Luke—Criticism, interpretation, ets. 2. Bible.
N.T. Gospels—Criticism, interpretation, ets. 3. Bible—Inspiration. I. Title.
BS2595.2R47- 1983   226'.406   83-13187
ISBN 0-8163-0542-0

Introduction

"All scripture is inspired by God." (2 Timothy 3:16). This statement is familiar to all readers of the Bible. It is appealed to in defense of the Bible's authority and origin. Some even appeal to the unique word in this verse that is translated "inspired" by the RSV, *theopneustos*—"God breathed"—as proof that the words of the Bible came directly from God.

Seventh-day Adventists, however, have gone on record in their official publications as rejecting "verbal inspiration." How, then, do we understand the process by which God gave us the Bible? To answer this question, 2 Peter 1:20, 21 is usually quoted, "First of all you must understand this, that no prophecy of scripture is a matter of one's own interpretation, because no prophecy ever came by the impulse of man, but men moved by the Holy Spirit spoke from God." Then this passage from 2 Peter is promptly misquoted. "You see," we are told, "the Bible was produced in exactly this way, 'men moved by the Holy Spirit spoke from God.' "

But Peter is speaking of prophecy in this passage. He informs us as to how prophecy originated. What about those books in the Bible that are not prophetic books, for example, Matthew, Mark, Luke, John, Acts, 1 and 2 Kings, 1 and 2 Chronicles? How did they come into being, and why do we consider them inspired? What about the portions of the books we call prophetic books that are not prophecy? For example, the historical sections of Daniel, Isaiah, Jeremiah? They are not prophecy. How did these portions come into being, and why do we consider them inspired?

Paul's statement in 2 Timothy is true! "All scripture is inspired by God." God is the source of each book in the canon of scripture, whether it is prophecy, history, poetry, or wisdom sayings. But Peter's statement only deals with prophecy! When we try to use the prophetic model described by Peter to account for all the books of the inspired canon, we immediately run into serious problems. The prophetic model cannot account for the origin of every book in the Bible. In fact there are a large number of books for which it cannot account. Therefore, we need a second model of inspiration to stand side by side with the prophetic model. A second model that will be a companion to and a complement of the prophetic model.

Where do we find such a model? Within the Bible itself! Actually, the Bible does not tell us very much about how it was put together. There are a few isolated statements such as the ones we quoted from 2 Timothy and 2 Peter. Of these few statements, one clearly identifies and describes how this second model of inspiration works, but we have virtually ignored it. That is why we try to use Peter's statement on prophecy to explain the origin of all biblical books, whether they are prophecy or not.

The purpose of this book is threefold: (1) to introduce the reader to the second model of inspiration, (2) to define it in such a way that it will become a tool to help us understand the message of the nonprophetic books, and (3) to give sufficient examples of how the authors of nonprophetic books worked under this second model so this model will be adequately and properly understood.

Contents

The Missing Link

The truth struck me like a bolt of lightning. I was teaching a religion class at Atlantic Union College in the early 70s. The general topic being discussed was the inspiration of the Bible, and on that day a Bible writer's use of quotations dominated the class period.

I can remember being deeply interested in individual reactions to the issue. Some students believed that inspired writer "A" would only quote from another inspired writer, say, inspired writer "B." This was the only way, they reasoned, that the quotation used from writer "B" could possibly be considered inspired. Other students disagreed. They believed that inspired writer "A" could quote from uninspired writer "B." Because "A" was inspired, the uninspired material quoted from writer "B" would now be considered inspired and authoritative.

Still others were not quite sure what they did believe on this point because they had never really thought it through. Then a young man raised his hand. He stated that his father was a pastor (his father and I had been fellow pastors in the New England area) and that his father had always taught, and still taught, that anything a "prophet" wrote was original. Therefore, divine inspiration made no allowance for quotations from other sources. It was then that the lightning struck!

Although some members of the class were amused at such an idea, the student was dead serious, and I was shocked. Shocked into the realization that many of our people (some pastors included) have a very limited understanding of inspiration. I sensed at that moment how vulnerable this student was. What would have happened to him if he had been confronted with certain facts about inspiration within a hostile environment? Would he have been able to maintain his faith in the Scriptures? It was fortunate for him that he was faced with this issue in a controlled environment that was friendly.

Misunderstandings concerning inspiration extend far beyond the use of quotations. Frederick E. J. Harder sensed the dangers as he pinpointed a second area of misunderstanding. "Traditionally, Seventh-day Adventists have tended toward the rather rigid position of John Calvin. Although official publications deny acceptance of the dogma of verbal inspiration, frequently there is a lack of understanding as to the full implications of the denial and a failure to replace it with a more consistent, realistic position. We cannnot with impunity continue to ignore the problems involved. There needs to be a frank recognition of issues accompanied by courageous effort toward their solution."[1]

If Harder's concluding statement was true when he penned these words, they are surely just as true today. But a "frank recognition of issues" involved in inspiration is not easy to come by, even if one puts forth the "courageous effort toward their solution." As William G. Johnsson admits, "Defining inspiration is like catching a rainbow. When we have put forth our best efforts, there will remain an elusive factor, an element of mystery."[2]

The purpose of this book is not to remove the "element of mystery" that Johnsson speaks of, for no human can penetrate and comprehend that which has not been revealed by the Almighty. And indeed, there are "elements of mystery" in the experience we call inspiration. Rather it is the purpose of this work, by examining those things which have been revealed, to present "a frank recognition" of some of the issues involved in inspiration. The aim is to isolate and examine the missing link in the Seventh-day Adventist understanding of inspiration. This is not said arrogantly nor boastfully. But, no matter how painful it may be, and it will be painful for some, we must admit there is a missing link. The statement of the student in class, the works of Ron Numbers and Walter Rea, and the admission of Harder testify to it.

As Harder observes: "In other words, a doctrine of divine rev-

elation can effectively survive only in its entirety—not in fragments. It will be embalmed soon after any of its parts are down-
graded, ignored, or inordinately exalted.''[3] Recent events have
proved Harder's words prophetic. As a church we have been pur-
suing and developing in great detail one phase of inspiration,
while leaving its companion virtually unrecognized and unex-
plored. As a result we have a fragmented understanding of inspiration, and, as Harder predicted, we are reaping the result.

An examination of the material produced by Adventist writers
over the years on the topic of inspiration will show that our efforts
have centered on the "prophetic model." I am borrowing this
term from Paul Achtemeier. He shows how this understanding of
inspiration was rooted in the experience of the Old Testament
prophet, and how, for the Jew, this model met the test of inspiration, i.e., "words written by human hands whose ultimate source
is God himself." The prophetic model was then applied by the
Jews to the other sections of the Bible, e.g., poems, songs, histor-
ies, wisdom sayings, etc.[4] Achtemeier then adds, "Such an understanding of prophecy, and of the prophet as the model for understanding the inspiration of Scripture, continued its influence in
the Church through the Middle Ages and into the period of the
reformation. . . . This view of inspiration continues to dominate
the thinking of the conservative Christian scholars of our time,
and is probably also the model assumed by most people who are
untrained in theology."[5] As a church, the majority of us understand inspiration in this same way. The prophetic model becomes
a big umbrella under which we gather all of the books of the Bible.
But herein we err. All books in the Bible were not written according to the same model. To recognize this fact does not mean that a
person is not conservative in his view of inspiration, in spite of
what Achtemeier says.

Therefore, while using Achtemeier's term, I would like to
redefine it. By so doing room is made for a second model of inspiration, which as you will see is the complement to and companion
of the prophetic model. In this present study, the term "prophetic
model" will refer to divine revelation coming to the prophet
through dreams, visions, thought illumination as seen in the
psalms and the wisdom literature, and the recording of these

theophanies (divine manifestations) under the guidance of the Holy Spirit.

Achtemeier picks out Jeremiah as the most appropriate example of this model, although certainly John the revelator could also be classified as an appropriate example. Achtemeier says: "Of all the prophets, Jeremiah is perhaps the clearest example of the usefulness of the prophetic model for inspiration. The words that Jeremiah has to speak to Israel were put into his mouth by God himself (Jer. 1:9, 2:1), but even more, Jeremiah at one point is commanded to write down the words that God had dictated to him (36:1-4, 32). Here clearly, is a model that meets the test of inspiration: words written by human hands whose ultimate source is God himself."[6] (We must not misunderstand Achtemeier here; he is not a defender of verbal inspiration.)

As Achtemeier correctly points out, the origin of all biblical books is commonly thought of as being classed under the umbrella of the prophetic model. As I have noted above, Adventist writers speak and think in these terms. The result is the fragmenting of inspiration.

Our literary productions on the topic of inspiration have been apologetic (the vindication of a position) and polemic (the refutation of the opinions of another). In our early years small books and pamphlets were produced that vindicated the Bible as the word of God. Fulfilled prophecy and archaeological finds became the proof of the Bible's origin and authority. These books were used widely in evangelism.

In recent years we have found it necessary to restate and carefully define inspiration for our own people. This necessity has arisen from recent attacks upon the work of Ellen G. White and has forced our restatements to be polemic. Because we accept Ellen White's visions as genuine, the prophetic model has been sharpened and further clarified under these attacks. However, these polemical works have not examined nor developed the second model of inspiration—the subject of this presentation. All Scripture is still classified under a common umbrella—the prophetic model.

For example, Harder sees the danger of fragmenting divine revelation as well as the danger of not accepting it in its entirety. By placing all Scripture within the prophetic model and ignoring the second, complementary model, he himself has not escaped the very danger he identified. "Beginning with events related to the Exodus and continuing to the close of the apostolic age, inspired revelations were committed to writing and 'embodied' in an inspired book."[7] The statement "Inspired revelations were committed to writing" fits the prophetic model. Harder paraphrases Ellen White here.[8] She is preparing her readers to understand that she has seen in vision (prophetic model) scenes from the great controversy between Christ and Satan. Therefore, the primary context in Ellen White's statement is the prophetic model of inspiration. However, Harder is not speaking only in terms of the prophetic books which resulted from divine revelations, rather, he is speaking of the entire canon of Scripture. Everything is included under the broad term "inspired-revelations." But there are many books in the Bible with which "inspired revelations" (as this expression is used by Harder and understood by Adventist readers) have no connection. These books did not result from dreams and visions. Strictly speaking they do not fit within the "prophetic model." One might legitimately ask, Where, then, do they fit? The answer is simple. They fit under the second, and neglected, model of inspiration.

When we come to the New Testament, Paul's statements are often set forth as an example of inspiration. For instance, he assures his readers—by using the term *theopneustos* (2 Timothy 3:16), which literally means "God breathed"—that Scripture is indeed inspired by God. Paul himself speaks of his own experience in the following words, "I did not receive it from man, nor was I taught it, but it came through a revelation of Jesus Christ." Galatians 1:12.

When one reads the use made of Paul by Adventist writers on inspiration, one is impressed that Paul and his revelations (prophetic model) are the norm for all the writings in the New Testament.[9] But we must not jump to such a hasty conclusion. Of all the New Testament writers only Paul and John are known to have had visions, and thus fit into the prophetic model. Paul only appeals to his visions in a limited way; and of the five New Testament books written by John only one originated from visions.

Therefore, it would seem that neither Paul's nor John's visions are the norm for New Testament books.

In the "Study Documents on Inspiration and Creation," published in the *Adventist Review* of January 17, 1980, we see the same approach to inspiration. "The Bible came through divine activity by which God revealed Himself to specially chosen agents. . . . God inspired these men to receive and communicate His revelation accurately and authoritatively."[10] Again we see all of Scripture being gathered together within the prophetic model, and no distinction made between those writings that resulted from direct revelations from God and those that did not. Here is where the problem lies.

Nearly forty years ago, Carlyle B. Haynes briefly touched upon the second model of inspiration in his apologetic work, *The Bible, Is It True?* Haynes said that part of the work of an inspired writer was "to compile and edit existing documents."[11] However, he expanded no further on this statement.

Except for a limited treatment found in the *Seventh-day Adventist Bible Commentary* on Luke 1:1-4,[12] it has only been recently that a few Adventist writers have begun to allude to the second model of inspiration. But none of them develops in detail how this model works. R. F. Cottrell remarked, "Aspects of Scripture that reflect the human element include: the selection of material and the order in which it is presented, the composition, the forms of expression. . . . The order is not always exact."[13] However, we shall soon see that under the second model of inspiration these characteristics are not merely "human elememts." They reflect the guidance of the Holy Spirit.

Warren H. Johns recognizes that the message of a Bible writer will "be shaped according to the messenger's thought patterns, culture, environment, background, training, personality, and reading habits."[14] Johns further says that "inspiration is not to be equated with originality," that it is "not diminished by the use of uninspired sources," and that "inspiration goes beyond what has been presented in vision, and sometimes stands independent of visions."[15] But all of this is said in the context of polemics. It is said in defense of the prophetic gift as exercised by Ellen White, who is thought of by many as writing according to the prophetic model. Therefore, these comments are equated with the prophetic model and are not permitted to stand on their own as characteristics of the second model of inspiration.

The "Study Documents on Inspiration and Creation" also alludes to a point that is characteristic of the second model of inspiration. "At times they [prophets who received dreams and visions] were divinely led to include material previously written that was relevant to their message."[16] But it is clear from the context that the authors of this document were thinking solely in terms of the prohetic model. The time is long overdue for us to think in terms of both models being present in the work of an inspired writer. Indeed, many Bible writers demonstrate this to be true. Attempting to include everything within one model has placed us in a vulnerable position.

If both models had been developed together as companions, one complementing the other, the charges of plagiarism leveled at Ellen White today may not have arisen. However, the prophetic model has been used to defend the gift bestowed upon the Seventh-day Adventist Church to such an extent that an unbalanced, one-sided view regarding inspiration has emerged. Actually, as an inspired writer, Ellen White worked under both models. More will be said about this at the conclusion of the next chapter.

It is not until we get to Robert W. Olson[17] and Roger W. Coon[18] (who quotes Olson) that the prologue to the Gospel of Luke (1:1-4) is taken seriously. And even at that, the reference to Luke is brief.

The most recent statement (at the time of writing this chapter) that deals with the second model of inspiration is found in an insert that appeared in *Ministry*, "The Truth About the White Lie." It occupies two paragraphs and reads as follows:

"The amount of borrowing is not the most important question however. An instructive parallel is found in the relationship of the Gospels. More than 90 percent of the Gospel of Mark is paralleled by passages in Matthew and Luke. Even so, contemporary critical Biblical scholars are coming more and more to the conclusion that although Matthew, Mark, and Luke used common materials, each was a distinct author in his own right. Thus even 'higher critics' have a more analytical approach to the study of literary sources than does *The White Lie*.

"At one time in the infancy of 'source criticism' the gospel writers were thought by higher critics to be little more than 'scissors and paste' plagiarizers. Now critical scholars realize that literary studies are not complete until they move beyond cataloging parallel passages to the more significant question of how the borrowed material was used by each author to make his own unique statement."[19]

Obviously, these two paragraphs are located in a much larger statement that is polemic in nature. Except for the brief treatment of Luke 1:1-4 in the commentary, this is, to my knowledge, the most detailed statement on the second model of inspiration.[20] Because this article is intended to answer the major issues raised by Rea, once more the second model of inspiration is not developed. In this case the reader can understand why.

Neither would anyone, reading Olson and Coon, realize that here, in Luke's prologue, lies the description of the second model of inspiration. Because Luke alone tells us how this model works, I have chosen to refer to it as "the Lucan model of inspiration." Here is the companion to the prophetic model; here is the missing link. Without it our teaching on inspiration is not presented "in its entirety." Without it our understanding is fragmented.

Now that we have identified the missing link, we must describe it.

References

1. Frederick E. J. Harder, "A Reply to Dr. Weiss," *Spectrum,* 7 (Autumn 1975): 57.

2. William G. Johnsson, "How does God speak?" *Ministry,* 54 (October 1981): 4.

3. Frederick E. J. Harder, "Divine Revelation: A Review of Some of Ellen G. White's Concepts," *Spectrum,* 2 (Autumn 1970): 54.

4. Paul J. Achtemeier, *The Inspiration of Scripture: Problems and Proposals* (Philadelphia: Westminster Press, 1980), p. 30.

5. *Ibid.,* pp. 31, 32.

6. *Ibid.,* p. 31.

7. Harder, p. 39.

8. Ellen G. White, *The Great Controversy Between Christ and Satan* (Mountain View, Calif.: Pacific Press Publishing Association, 1911), p. v.

9. Cf. Jean R. Zurcher, "I Believe . . . in the Bible as the Inspired Word of God," *Review and Herald,* October 14, 1971, p. 6; Raoul Dederen, "Toward a Seventh-day Adventist Theology of Revelation-Inspiration," in *A Symposium on Biblical Hermeneutics,* ed. Gordon M. Hyde (Washington D.C.: Biblical Research Committee, 1974), p. 14.

10. "Study Documents on Inspiration and Creation," *Adventist Review,* January 17, 1980, p. 9.

11. Carlyle B. Haynes, *The Bible, Is It True?* (Washington, D.C.: Review and Herald Publishing Association, 1946), p. 51.

12. *The Seventh-day Adventist Bible Commentary* (Washington D.C.: Review and Herald Publishing Association, 1956), 5:668-670.

13. R. F. Cottrell, "The Word Became Scripture," *Review and Herald,* April 28, 1977, p. 17.

14. Warren H. Johns, "Ellen White: Prophet or Plagiarist?" *Ministry* 55 (June 1982): 17.

15. *Ibid.,* p. 17.

16. "Study Documents on Inspiration and Creation," p. 9.

17. Robert W. Olson, *One Hundred and One Questions on the Sanctuary and on Ellen White* (Washington, D.C.: Ellen G. White Estate, 1981), pp. 105-107.

18. Roger W. Coon, "Inspiration/Revelation: What It Is and How It Works, Part I, The Prophetic Gift in Operation," *Journal of Adventist Education,* 44 (October-November 1981): 24.

19. "The Truth About the White Lie," *Ministry,* 55 (August 1982): 2.

20. Since the writing of this chapter, an article by Delmer A. Johnson has appeared in the *Adventist Review* (December 30, 1982), entitled, "The Sources of Inspired Writings." Johnson deals in some detail with the issue of common sources used by Old Testament writers who did not receive dreams and visions. As one of Johnson's former teachers, I am gratified to see him making a contribution in this neglected area.

The Lucan Model

Many serious readers of the gospel accounts of Jesus' life and ministry will sooner or later arrive at a number of conclusions. Three of these conclusions will be these: (1) Each gospel writer saw Jesus from a different perspective and was eager to communicate his understanding of Jesus to his readers. (2) In order to achieve this goal, different aspects of the gospel story were emphasized by the four gospel writers. (Each writer painted a faithful portrait of the Saviour, but each added different highlights.) (3) The prophetic model of inspiration (dreams and visions) is inadequate to explain the variations in the gospel portrait.

If the prophetic model is claimed as the source for the gospel account of Jesus' ministry, the reader can only conclude that God was inconsistent with the information He gave to the gospel writers. Knowing that God is not inconsistent, the only other conclusion the reader can come to is that Matthew, Mark, Luke, and John worked under a model of inspiration that was different from the prophetic model. What has been said here about the four gospels can also be said of 1 and 2 Kings, 1 and 2 Chronicles, and other Old Testament books. The evidence that lies behind these conclusions will be examined as we proceed from this point.

Each year I teach a class in the theological seminary at Andrews University called the theology of the synoptic Gospels (Matthew, Mark, and Luke). The very fist day of each new session I tell the class that, if they are going to understand what the synoptic writers are saying theologically, they must understand how the Gospels are put together. Why? Because the synoptic

Gospels are an expression of the writers' theological understanding of the Christ-event, and this expression is orchestrated by the way the Gospels are constructed. Once this has been stated, we spend the next several days examining Luke's prologue (1:1-4) where the Lucan model of inspiration is defined.

The importance of the prologue to Luke's Gospel cannot be emphasized enough. Alfred Plummer, a well-known commentator on Luke, says, "This prologue contains all that we really *know* respecting the composition of early narratives of the life of Christ, and it is the test by which theories as to the origin of our Gospels must be judged. No hypothesis is likely to be right which does not harmonize with what is told us here."[1] Sensing the truth of Plummer's statement, we now face the task of understanding what Luke tells us about the composition of his Gospel. What we learn here can then be applied to the remaining Gospels and other biblical books that do not fall under the prophetic model.

The prologue reads as follows, "Inasmuch as many have undertaken to compile a narrative of the things which have been accomplished among us, just as they were delivered to us by those who from the beginning were eyewitnesses and ministers of the word, it seemed good to me also, having followed all things closely for some time past, to write an orderly account for you, most excellent Theophilus, that you may know the truth concerning the things of which you have been informed." Luke 1:1-4.

I am sure that you, as well as I, know from experience that what a statement *does not say* is just as important as what it *does say*. This is indeed the case with Luke's prologue. First of all, what does the prologue *not* say? (1) Luke does not claim dreams nor visions as the source for his Gospel. (2) He does not claim to be an eyewitness to the life and ministry of Jesus. In fact, he separates himself from those who were. (3) If you read these four verses carefully, it appears that Luke does not claim to have taken his information from previously written sources. (This is an issue that we cannot get into here. However, because Luke is aware of the "many" who have already written gospels, we will assume for the time being that he had also read them.)

If Luke did not receive from dreams and visions what we find in his Gospel, and if he was not an eyewitness to Jesus' ministry, where did he get his information, and how did inspiration work in his case? These two questions can be answered by examining what Luke *does* say in his prologue.

1. "Many" followers of Jesus had undertaken the task of recording what had happened through the divine activity of God. Verse 1. Luke gives us no clue as to how many authors this involved, but the number may have been considerable. We can no longer hold to the notion that only four Gospels were produced by the followers of Jesus.

Another notion that has dominated scholarly circles for well over a century is seriously challenged by Luke 1:1. New Testament scholars have long believed that the Gospel of Mark and an unknown book of Jesus' teachings (commonly referred to as "Q") were the sources of information for the writing of Matthew and Luke. However, Luke 1:1 would seem to argue against this idea. "Many" would certainly be more than Mark and Q! Because Luke is aware of the existence of "many" gospels, he probably had read them. This seems to be supported by what he says in verse 3, where he tells us that he had "followed" everything concerning the life of Jesus carefully. To do this, Luke would want to call on every source of information that was available to him.

The impression one gains from Luke 1:1 is that there was a flurry of writing activity at a crucial point in the history of the Christian church. This crucial point was reached when eyewitnesses began to die off and the early Christians began to realize there would be a delay in the coming of the Bridegroom. Therefore, "many" recorded the stories of Jesus' miracles and His teachings as they remembered the accounts from the eyewitnesses. It was at this point that Luke decided to write what he had learned about Jesus. Ray Summers says, "By the time of his [Luke's] writing, Gospel-writing had become an established practice. . . . The desire of the people to know the works and words of Jesus resulted in many attempts at Gospel-writing."[2]

Although Luke was familiar with the "many" gospels that preceded the writing of his book, we know nothing of them today. They have been lost, and only God knows if any of them will be found again. However, as we read the Gospel of Luke, we are probably reading many statements that were in these other gospels. This brings us to the next point stressed in Luke's prologue.

2. Luke says that those who were eyewitnesses and ministers of the word delivered the information about Jesus to us. Four questions raised by this statement need to be examined: (1) Who were the eyewitnesses, (2) who were the ministers of the word, (3) what can we learn from the word *delivered,* and (4) who were the "us"?

First, who were the eyewitnesses? The answer to this is the simplest of the four questions just asked. The eyewitnesses would be any who heard Jesus preach or saw His deeds. This would include the apostles, the seventy disciples, the women who attended Jesus, members of the crowds who followed Him, people who were healed, and members of His family, i.e., His mother Mary, His brothers and sisters. All of these people, at some time or other, bore their testimony as eyewitnesses. It is probably true that Luke did not have personal interviews with them all, but everything that Luke records he received in some way from others.

Second, who were the ministers of the word? Willard Swartley builds a convincing argument that these ministers of the word, called *hupēretai,* were individuals that performed a special function in the early church. He theorizes that they were specially chosen to memorize the sermons, parables, and deeds of Jesus. Their responsibility was to repeat from memory what the Lord said and did, and possibly to interpret their meaning. Swartley proposes that John Mark was one of these "ministers of the word" and that Mark was taken by Paul on the first missionary tour because of the contribution he could make to the preaching of the gospel.[3] There is seeming confirmation for this conclusion. When speaking of this first missionary tour, Luke identifies John Mark as a *hupēretēs* in Acts 13:5.

If Swartley's position is correct, some very interesting possibilities arise. For example, scholars have recognized for years that there is a very close literary relationship between Luke and Mark. It has been assumed that Luke had the Gospel of Mark before him and used it as the basis for his own Gospel. Thus, they reason, Luke borrowed (copied) large segments of Mark while working into his Gospel information he took from other sources, e.g., from Q, the hypothetical, non-Marcan source, and from material not found in Mark and Matthew (commonly identified by the letter L).

However, following Swartley's suggestion and taking at face value what Luke says about his own Gospel in his prologue, the following scenario can be constructed: As a minister of the word (*hupēretēs*), Mark had memorized a large number of the deeds and teachings of Jesus. Plummer is convinced that Luke personally knew Mark. "He [Luke] certainly was acquainted with S. Mark, who was perhaps already preparing material for his own Gospel when he and S. Luke were with the Apostle [Paul] in Rome (Col. iv. 10, 14; Philem. 24)."[4]

Mark repeated from memory for Luke what he knew about Jesus' ministry. Mark then also put into writing what he knew as a *hupēretēs*. Thus we have the Gospel of Mark. Luke jotted down what he heard from Mark and supplemented it with what he could learn from other ministers of the word (*hupēretai*), eyewitnesses, and the "many" gospels that had been written.

Because Mark came to be highly esteemed by Paul (2 Timothy 4:11) and because of Paul's close relationship with and influence on Luke, Mark's oral report of Jesus' ministry was accepted as completely trustworthy, and thus it became the foundation for Luke's Gospel. This can account for the close literary similarities between Mark an Luke, while at the same time remain true to Luke's statement that he received his information through oral interviews with eyewitnesses and ministers of the word. Which takes us to the next point.

Third, Luke stresses that the information he received from the eyewitnesses and the ministers of the word was received by oral transmission. He says, "Just as they were delivered to us by those who from the beginning were eyewitnesses and ministers of the word." Verse 2. The Greek word *paredosan*, translated "delivered," is derived from one of two words, *paradidōmi* and *paralambanō*, that had become technical terms in the New Testament for the transmission of oral teaching. Therefore, when either or both of these words appear within the context of teaching, we can understand them to refer to oral instruction or oral transmission of information. This insight into the word *delivered* supports our scenario.

Finally, who were the "us" Luke referred to? The eyewitnesses and ministers of the word delivered (orally) to "us" the information about Jesus. "Us" naturally included Luke, who was about to write his Gospel. But who else would it include? The only other people Luke has spoken of, other than the eyewitnesses and the ministers of the word, are the "many." Therefore, these earlier gospel writers received their information about Jesus just as Luke did, i.e., through oral interviews with eyewitnesses and ministers of the word.

3. This now leaves us with Luke's stated intentions found in verse 3 of his prologue: "It seemed good to me also, having followed all things closely for some time past, to write an orderly account for you, most excellent Theophilus."

If Luke was not an eyewitness of Jesus' ministry, how is it possible for him to follow all things "closely"? He did so by compiling information about Jesus from every source available. And, as we have seen, he even tells us where he derived his information. He got it from the "many" gospels that had been written, from eyewitnesses, and from the ministers of the word.

By looking at what Luke wrote, we even know when the "beginning" started. Immediately after the prologue, we are introduced to Zachariah and Elizabeth. Here is the beginning of the gospel story for Luke, i.e., the announcement of the coming birth of John the Baptist.

One more very important thing we need to note before we leave Luke's prologue. Luke tells Theophilus that he is going to write an orderly account. This statement is generally understood to mean a chronological account of Jesus' ministry. However, when one begins to read Luke, he becomes aware there are a number of events that are not in the same order as they are in Matthew and Mark. Of course, it may be argued that Luke has them in the correct order and that they are out of order in Matthew and Mark. This argument could be taken seriously if it were not for the fact that what appears out of order in Luke fits thematically with that which Luke is developing concerning Jesus. Therefore, one is forced to the conclusion that Luke is not speaking of a chronological order in his prologue.

As we get into our study we shall see several events in Jesus' life that are moved around chronologically by Luke and other gospel writers for the purpose of developing certain themes. To recognize this fact goes a long way toward helping to understand the Lucan model of inspiration.

When people come to realize that many of the events in Jesus' ministry have been moved out of their historical sequence, some begin to fear that perhaps the Gospels are not historically accurate. This is a needless fear. First of all, each event recorded by the gospel writers did take place historically. Second, using historical events in connection with other historical happenings to establish a truth about Jesus or to illustrate a spiritual teaching He was presenting, does not make these events unhistorical, even if they are presented out of chronological sequence.

This is done repeatedly by preachers, and no one thinks anything of it. As they present God's word from the pulpit, ministers frequently make references to historical events recorded in various places in the Bible without regard to their chronological sequence. The preacher does not remind his congregation what the historical sequence of these events are. Nor does the congregation require that this be done. If an event from the life of Moses follows an event from the life of Elijah as a sermon illustration, everyone in the audience knows that this does not render these events unhistorical. Rather, historical events are called upon to establish and illustrate spiritual truth. This is exactly what the gospel writers did as authors and theologians.

If the reader is interested in possible solutions to what Luke meant by "orderly account," I suggest he consult some Bible commentaries in order to find the various views that are offered. There is no need to digress to pursue these views here.

What are the implications of Luke's prologue for the topic of inspiration? First of all, Luke received the information that he records for us from sources other than dreams and visions. His sources are quite human—eyewitnesses, ministers of the word, and previously written gospels. In other words, the Lucan model of inspiration is based on research—reading and oral interviews.

How does inspiration work when the inspired writer relies solely on research? Another inspired writer solves the problem for us. Ellen White says: "God has been pleased to communicate

His truth to the world by human agencies, and He Himself, by His Holy Spirit, qualified men and enabled them to do this work. He guided the mind in the selection of what to speak and what to write.''[5]

This statement seems especially suited to the Lucan model of inspiration, i.e., the Spirit guided the mind of the gospel writers in the selection of material to write. Other statements made by Ellen White are also helpful. She indicates that God used the background, training, education, and interests of the various Bible writers as means of bringing to the human family the various aspects of the plan of redemption.[6]

There is one more very important fact about the Lucan model of inspiration that needs to be stated. Perhaps the best way to do it is to construct another scenario. If we could have looked in on Luke as he was about to write his Gospel, we would have seen him sitting at his desk, with papyrus or parchment note cards standing in piles all over the desk. On these cards information had been collected that would be considered for inclusion in his Gospel. Some cards contained direct quotes from earlier gospels, while others contained accounts of eyewitnesses who saw Jesus perform miracles. Still other cards contained parables and sermons as they were reported to him by people who heard Jesus. Several piles of cards would contain quotations from Mark, who orally reported to Luke what Jesus had said and done. Then there were cards that contained oral reports from other *hupēretai* (ministers of the word).

As Luke began to sift through the piles of cards, he thought of Theopilus, the Gentile to whom this Gospel was destined when it reached its finished form. Luke wanted Theophilus to see Jesus as he saw Him, to understand Jesus as he understood Him.

As Luke began to write, the Holy Spirit quietly impressed him as to what miracles to choose, what parables would illustrate the points that Luke wanted Theophilus to understand. Cards were rearranged. Some were set aside because what they reported was not as significant to Luke as others. Some of the cards that contained quotations from Mark were reworked by Luke. He added a point here, changed a phrase there. He even omitted bits of information that did not seem relevant. These changes in

Mark's account were based upon additional information that Luke gleaned from eyewitnesses and other ministers of the word. Luke even changed the order of some events reported by Mark so the point he was developing might be seen more clearly by Theophilus. We have been told by Ellen White that the miracles of Jesus are not in their exact order. Rather, they were used by the gospel writers as literary devices to illustrate a developing point or to stress a truth the writers wished their readers to see.[7]

As Luke worked under the guidance of the Holy Spirit, a portrait of Jesus began to take shape, a portrait that is quite similar to the one developed by Matthew and Mark, yet different. It was Luke's portrait. It was a picture of Jesus as Luke saw Him, as Luke understood Him. Yet all the while, the Spirit worked with Luke's interests, his education, his background. The portrait of Jesus that Luke developed is one that God not ony wanted Theophilus to see, but one He wanted all followers of Jesus to see until the end of time.

In order to comprehend the Lucan model of inspiration, we must recognize that the Bible writer who operated under this model was an author and a theologian in his own right. As an author he shaped and arranged the material he researched so that the end product expressed his interests. As a theologian he worked with the material so that the end product expressed his theological understanding. Yet the Spirit guided throughout the whole process.

As we turn to the text of the synoptic Gospels, we must ever keep in mind these important points in the Lucan model. Only then can we begin to see what Luke, Matthew, and Mark, as individual authors and theologians, are telling us about Jesus. If we do not keep these points in mind, we lose the portrait of Jesus as it is developed by each writer.

What follows is said at the risk of redundancy, but there must be no misunderstanding. Simply because Matthew, Mark, Luke, John, and other New and Old Testament writers did not receive dreams and visions, does not mean that their writings are less authoritative than those written under the prophetic model. Nor does it mean that these writings are less inspired. The Holy Spirit was actively engaged in both models. The results of both models worked to fulfill God's purpose. In other words this was a collection of writings produced under His guidance that would be the chart and compass for His people as they journey toward their heavenly homeland.

Because research, which necessarily involves quoting and gleaning ideas and concepts from others, is the basis of the Lucan model, this does not mean that all researchers are inspired in the sense that the biblical writers who wrote under this model were inspired. God was working in and through these men to accomplish a special task which was vital to the success of His cause throughout the generations of time.

Seventh-day Adventists believe that the spirit of prophecy—one of the spiritual gifts—was bestowed on Ellen White for the guidance of their church in the closing days of earth's history. A study of her writings shows that they exhibit both the prophetic and the Lucan models of inspiration. Given visions of biblical and post-biblical historical events, she read widely concerning what had been revealed to her. As she wrote about these events, she often used what she had gathered from uninspired sources to help explain and describe what she had been shown.

In his book *The White Lie* Walter Rea seems to realize that an understanding and acceptance of the Lucan model of inspiration would destroy the foundation upon which his criticisms of Ellen White are based. He therefore attempts to belittle those who defend Ellen White's use of the Lucan model. Says Rea: "After all, it had been done before—or so the modern defenders of the Adventist faith were to propound some one hundred thirty years later. It came to be said that St. Luke copied from St. Mark and that Paul was sneaking material from the Greeks without even letting them know. John the Revelator was stealing from ancient pagans for his ideas, and Jude did a test run from early pseudepigraphical works. Even Moses, instead of lifting the Ten Commandments from God, is said to have taken them from Hammurabi, an ancient lawgiver, or even others before his time."[8]

But the facts are clear. Inspired biblical writers did do research. They did quote ("borrow" or "copy"), both from other biblical writers and nonbiblical writers.

Leaving all of this for the time being, let us see how the gospel writers functioned under the Lucan model of inspiration.

References

1. Alfred Plummer, *A Critical and Exegetical Commentary of the Gospel According to S. Luke* (Edinburgh: T & T Clark, 1913), p. 2.

2. Ray Summers, *Commentary on Luke* (Waco, Tex.: Word Books, 1972), p. 19.

3. Willard M. Swartley, *Mark: The Way For All Nations* (Scottdale, Penn.: Herald Press, 1981), p. 28.

4. Plummer, p. xxiii.

5. Ellen G. White, *The Great Controversy Between Christ and Satan* (Mountain View, Calif.: Pacific Press Publishing Association, 1911), p. vi.

6. *Ibid.*

7. Ellen G. White, *Selected Messages* (Washington, D.C.: Review and Herald Publishing Association, 1958), bk. 1, p. 20.

8. Walter T. Rea, *The White Lie* (Turlock, Calif.: M & R Publications, 1982), p. 46.

Gospel Writers as Authors

Once a person becomes aware of the Lucan model, he finds himself reading the Gospels differently from the way he has read them before. He catches himself asking such questions as these: Why did Luke record this event at this point in Jesus' ministry, when Matthew and Mark have the very same event in an entirely different sequence? Or, when he has read an account in Matthew, he finds himself yielding to the irresistible urge to turn to Mark and to see how Mark records the same story. He may even be surprised to find that Mark does not record it at all. Then the question comes to mind, what is Matthew telling me about Jesus by recording this story, and what is Mark telling me by leaving it out? The fact that Matthew has the story and Mark does not is not an accident. Not only this, but it does not mean that Mark did not know the story. This is just another example, among scores of examples, of the gospel writers working as individual authors and theologians. They are simply being used by the Holy Spirit as He wills as they put their personal touch to the portrait of Jesus.

We have finally reached the point where we can take a detailed look at examples of how the Lucan model of inspiration works. The synoptic Gospels will be the laborabory within which we will work. They are replete with examples of what we have been describing. It is obviously impossible to examine every one of them. Therefore, we will take a sampling of several specimens that range from simple word omission/addition to the complete rewriting of an event and the rearrangement of content. Remember, all of this was done under the guidance and superintendence of the Holy Spirit, and the results are just as divinely inspired and authoritative as anything written by the Bible writers under the prophetic model.

Let us begin with the first event in Jesus' Galilean ministry as it is recorded by the three synoptic writers. Have you ever noticed that Matthew begins Jesus' ministry with the call of the first disciples, and then he goes on to record the Sermon on the Mount? Mark, on the other hand, begins with the call of the first disciples. This is followed by the healing of the demoniac in the synagogue at Capernaum. If we were to stop at this point and go no further, it is obvious that the prophetic model is incapable of explaining what has happened. If, for instance, we claim the prophetic model here, we would have to say that God, through visions, showed Matthew and Mark two distinct events, each one of which was the starting point of Jesus' ministry. In other words, when Jesus entered Galilee and called his disciples, did this particular phase of His ministry begin with the Sermon on the Mount or with he healing of the demoniac? If one insists that the prophetic model alone is the source of the Gospels, it would appear that God was not sure whether Jesus' ministry began with the Sermon on the Mount or the healing of the demoniac. Or, one could conclude that, if He showed Matthew that it was the Sermon on the Mount, He had forgotten this fact when He gave the vision of the demoniac to Mark.

When we turn to Luke the issue becomes even more complicated. Luke does not record the call of the first disciples at the beginning of the Galilean ministry. He starts his Gospel with a third event that is entirely different from Matthew and Mark. Luke begins the Galilean ministry with Jesus' visit to Nazareth, which includes the reading of the Isaiah scroll in the synagogue and the attempt of the townspeople to kill Jesus. In Luke, several events precede the call of the disciples which in Mark follow this call. In other words, according to Mark's account the disciples were with Jesus when these events occurred, while in Luke Jesus had not yet called them. Perhaps things can be more easily visualized if we list these events as recorded by the three synoptic writers.

Matthew	Mark	Luke
Introductory statement to Galilean ministry (4:12-17)	Introductory statement to Galilean ministry (1:14, 15)	Introductory statement to Galilean ministry (4:14, 15)
Call of first disciples (4:18-22)	Call of first disciples (1:16-20)	
Summary statement on ministry (4:23-25)		
Sermon on the Mount (5-7)	Healing of the demoniac (1:21-28)	Visit to Nazareth (4:16-30)

What do we actually see here? We see three individual authors working under the Lucan model! By the order of events, each one is telling us something a little different about Jesus. Individual highlights in the portrait, if you please.

If you read the introductory statements in all three Gospels you will find them to be quite different. Even here, the writers add different highlights. However, we are interested in finding out why each writer begins Jesus' Galilean ministry with a different major event—Matthew with the Sermon on the Mount, Mark with the healing of the demoniac, and Luke with the visit to the synagogue in Nazareth. We shall look at the rearrangement of the call to discipleship within Luke at a later time.

An examination of John's Gospel shows us that Matthew, Mark, and Luke do not record the first year and a half of Jesus' ministry. John does this for us. If we were reading the synoptic Gospels alone, we would conclude that Jesus went directly into Galilee after His baptism and the temptations in the wilderness. But this is not the case. The synoptic writers jump over the first part of Jesus' ministry and pick it up as He enters the year-long ministry in Galilee.

Now, what are the synoptic writers telling us about Jesus? Let us begin with Matthew and the Sermon on the Mount. As you read this sermon carefully, you realize that Jesus is speaking a great deal about the kingdom of God. Kingdom language is present throughout. For example, "Blessed are the poor in spirit, for theirs is the kingdom of heaven." Matthew 5:3. "Blessed are the meek, for they shall inherit the earth." Matthew 5:5. "Blessed are the pure in heart, for they shall see God." Matthew 5:8. "Blessed are those who are persecuted for righteousness' sake, for theirs is the kingdom of heaven." Matthew 5:10. "For I tell you, unless your righteousness exceeds that of the scribes and Pharisees, you will never enter the kingdom of heaven." Matthew 5:20 "You have heard that it was said . . . . But I say . . . ." Matthew 5:21, 22, 27, 28, 31-34, 38, 39, 43, 44—showing Jesus' authority as King. "Our Father who art in heaven, hallowed be thy name. Thy kingdom come." Matthew 6:9, 10. "Not every one who says to me, 'Lord, Lord,' shall enter the kingdom of heaven, but he who does the will of my Father who is in heaven." Matthew 7:21. Besides these verses that specifically mention the kingdom, there are many more that deal with the ethics, the life-style of those who enter the kingdom.

Ellen White says of this sermon, "In the Sermon on the Mount He sought to undo the work that had been wrought by false education, and to give His hearers a right conception of His kingdom and of His own character."[1] Therefore, coming as it does in the Gospel of Matthew at the beginning of Jesus' ministry, this sermon becomes a proclamation as to the nature of the kingdom, the King who rules this kingdom, and the ethics of those who would become citizens of this kingdom.

But Matthew does not drop this sermon about the kingdom upon his readers with no prior preparation. He spends four chapters preparing them for the proclamation that is to be made by the Sermon on the Mount. Thus we see Matthew's intense interest in Jesus as Israel's King. Notice how he prepares his readers to accept this sermon as a proclamation of Jesus' kingship and His kingdom.

The very first words Matthew wrote are as follows, "The book of the genealogy of Jesus Christ, the son of David." Matthew 1:1. Neither Mark nor Luke begin their Gospels with such a clear statement regarding the relationship between Jesus and David. The phrase "Son of David" suggests Jesus' royal descent as the Messiah or King. Matthew immediately follows this statement of kingship with the genealogy of Jesus. In this ancestral line are listed the kings of Judah. Matthew 1:2-16. Luke also gives Jesus' genealogy, but there is not one king listed, except David. Whereas Jesus' genealogy is traced back through the kings to Solomon and then David in Matthew's Gospel, in Luke, Jesus' line goes back to Nathan (David's third son, 2 Sam. 5:14) then David. Again, the obvious emphasis in Matthew is on Jesus the King.

It is Matthew that records the visit of the wise men. When they arrive in Jerusalem, they ask, "Where is he who has been born king of the Jews?" Matthew 2:2. Some New Testament scholars think that Matthew recorded the visit of the wise men because he knew nothing about the visit of the shepherds to the manger. There are also those who think that Luke recorded the visit of the shepherds because he knew nothing about the arrival of the wise men. I do not believe this is the case. Rather, both Matthew and Luke were writing under the Lucan model of inspiration. As Matthew was sifting through his pile of note cards marked "nativity," he set aside those that recorded the visit of the shepherds and kept those that told the story of the wise men. Why? Because the visit of the shepherds had nothing to do with the issue of kingship, whereras the wise men came asking, "Where is he who has been born king of the Jews?"

The same can be said of Luke. He was not interested in Jesus' kingship at this point, so he set aside the cards that reported the visit of the wise men. However, in the visit of the shepherds Luke found something that deeply fascinated him—how the lowly and despised of society responded to Jesus as "Saviour." After all, did not the angel tell the shepherds while they were in the fields, "For to you is born this day in the city of David a Savior, who is Christ the Lord"? Luke 2:11.

Observe that in Matthew the visit of the wise men is immediately followed by the reaction of King Herod. "Where is the Christ to be born?" he demanded of the chief priests and scribes. See Matthew 2:4. When he found out, and then realized he had been spurned by the wise men, he dispatched his soldiers to execute the Prince. Why did Herod do this? He feared for his throne. He was determined not to give it up to anyone. The attempt to kill Jesus was rooted in the issue of kingship.

Matthew now hurries to the ministry of John the Baptist. This great prophet appears in the wilderness preaching, "Repent, for the kingdom of heaven is at hand." Matthew 3:2. Did you ever notice that John makes this proclamation about the kingdom of heaven only in Matthew's Gospel? Neither in Mark's Gospel nor in Luke's does John say anything about the kingdom being at hand. Is it because they did not know that John proclaimed such a message? No! At this point Matthew is interested in the kingdom and Jesus' kingship. Inclusion of John's proclamation helps Matthew develop this theme as he approaches the Sermon on the Mount.

Following His baptism, Jesus enters the wilderness and is tempted by Satan. Again notice how Matthew stresses the kingdom. Have you ever puzzled over the reasons why the three temptations pressed upon Jesus by Satan climax with the devil taking Jesus to a high mountain? The temptations in Luke climax with Jesus being taken to the pinnacle of the temple. Why are these last two temptations reversed by Matthew and Luke?

What is at stake in this last temptation as it appears in Matthew? "Again, the devil took him to a very high mountain, and showed him all the kingdoms of the world and the glory of them; and he said to him, 'All these I will give you, if you will fall down and worship me.' " Matthew 4:8, 9. The temptations in Matthew climax with the question as to who was going to rule the world. The issue is kingship! Luke, as we shall see, is concerned with release from Satan's power, so he concludes the temptations with Satan's leaving Jesus standing on the pinnacle of the temple.

With the words of the third temptation, as recorded by Matthew, "Begone, Satan! for it is written, 'You shall worship the Lord your God and him only shall you serve,' " the issue of who was to rule the world was settled forever. Therefore, before Matthew enters into the details of Jesus' ministry, the issue of Jesus' kingship is settled. As Matthew's readers follow Jesus through the passion to the cross, they know all will come out all right. Pilate's placard over the head of the dying Saviour speaks a truth, but it presents only a portion of the truth—"This is Jesus the King of the Jews." Matthew 27:37. Matthew's readers know there is a more profound truth in the identification of Jesus as King—the climax of the wilderness temptations has established that Jesus is King, not only of the Jews, but of the whole world.

But now returning to Matthew's introduction to Jesus' Galilean ministry, Matthew is not quite ready for the Sermon on the Mount. There is one more thing he wishes his readers to understand. We find it in his introductory statement to Jesus' Galilean ministry, which extends from chapter 4, verses 12 through 17. It is the longest introductory statement in the synoptic Gospels. But notice how this statement concludes, "From that time Jesus began to preach, saying, 'Repent, for the kingdom of heaven is at hand.' " Matthew 4:17.

Observe that this is the same announcement John the Baptist made in Matthew 3:2.

The verb "is at hand" is a Greek intensive perfect (ēggiken). It is recognized that as an intensive perfect verb it may be translated as an English present.[2] Therefore, we can understand Jesus to be saying, "Repent, for the kingdom of heaven is here." The idea of the present kingdom is stated again by Jesus at a later date: "But if it is by the Spirit of God that I cast out demons, then the kingdom of God has come upon you." Matthew 12:28.

Now that Matthew has established the fact that Jesus is King and that the kingdom has arrived, he introduces the Sermon on the Mount, which explains the nature of the kingdom, the nature of its King, and the ethics of those who wish to be citizens of the kingdom.

So we see Matthew working as an author. We now understand why Matthew opens the Galilean ministry with the Sermon on the Mount. We also see that as Matthew writes under the Lucan model he chooses material from his research that helps develop a portrait of Jesus that has Matthean highlights.

As one reads Mark's Gospel, it becomes very clear that Mark is a young man in a hurry. He says absolutely nothing about the nativity. He deals with the ministry of John the Baptist in only eight verses, the baptism of Jesus in three, and the temptations in the wilderness in two. This gives us a total of thirteen verses. Where is he going in such a rush? He wants to get to the Galilean ministry and so gives everything that preceded it a quick nod as he goes by.

Mark begins Jesus' ministry with the exorcism in the synagogue at Capernaum. He does not follow Matthew's sequence and present the Sermon on the Mount. What is Mark telling us about Jesus by beginning his Gospel this way?

First we must examine Mark's introductory summary statement on the Galilean ministry. Observe that all three synoptics have such a statement preceding the record of Jesus' ministry. In the typical style we have just noted, Mark has only two verses, but they are very important for his Gospel. They read as follows: "Now after John was arrested, Jesus came into Galilee, preaching the gospel of God, and saying, 'The time is fulfilled, and the kingdom of God is at hand; repent, and believe in the gospel.' " Mark 1:14, 15.

"The kingdom of God is at hand" (ēggiken) is the same statement recorded by Matthew. We must understand it in the same way as we did when studying Matthew's introductory statement, i.e., "the kingdom of God has arrived." Mark intensifies this truth by saying that Jesus added, "the time is fulfilled." These two statements side by side become an emphatic proclamation that the kingdom is here.

Matthew deals with the presence of the kingdom through the Sermon on the Mount. Mark has a flare for the dramatic. Following the introductory statement, Jesus calls the first four disciples (verses 16 to 20), as He does in Matthew; then we find Him in the synagogue at Capernaum (verses 21 to 28). While He was teaching, a demon-possessed man screamed out and confronted Jesus. The synagogue routine stopped. This is what Satan wanted. All attention was focused on the demoniac, who challenged, "What have you to do with us, Jesus of Nazareth?" Verse 24.

The people sat frozen in their seats. In utter disbelief they watched two supernatural powers in combat. "Have you come to destroy us? I know who you are, the Holy One of God" (verse 24), taunted the demon. The demon had disrupted Jesus' teaching and had diverted the attention of the people away from the truths He was presenting. Enough was enough! Jesus exorcised the demon—"Be silent, and come out of him." Verse 25. Obeying the command of Jesus, the demon left. In amazement the people said, "What is this? A new teaching! With authority he commands even the unclean spirits, and they obey him." Verse 27.

Why did Mark choose this miracle to begin the ministry of Jesus? Could it be tied to Jesus' statement in the summary that introduces the Galilean ministry, "The time is fulfilled, and the kingdom of God is at hand [is present]"? From the writings of the ancient rabbis we understand that they had been teaching the people that when the kingdom of God arrived and the Messiah had come, the kingdom of Satan would be vanquished. Everyone in the synagogue understood this.

In the confrontation between Jesus and the demoniac, the people saw acted out what they had been taught to watch for. No wonder they responded, "What is this? A new teaching!" The exorcism was a dramatic proclamation that Jesus is the Messiah and that the kingdom of God had arrived. Thus Jesus' words in Mark's introductory summary statement, "the time is fulfilled, and the kingdom of God is at hand," becomes programmatic, i.e., it outlines the ministry Jesus is to follow. The exorcism in the synagogue is a deed of proclamation in Mark, demonstrating to Mark's readers that Jesus is the Messiah and the kingdom has come.

In essence, Matthew and Mark are saying the same thing, but using two entirely different events. What does this tell us about the Lucan model? Individual authors can proclaim the same truth, but approach it from each one's point of individual interest by using available material that will fit their interests. This latitude to work with research material is a key characteristic of the Lucan model.

We now have Luke's report to investigate. Luke's introductory summary statement on the Galilean ministry is short, as is Mark's. But what a difference! "And Jesus returned in the power of the Spirit into Galilee, and a report concerning him went out through all the surrounding country. And he taught in their synagogues, being glorified by all." Luke 4:14, 15.

There is nothing in Luke's introductory statement about the kingdom being present as there is in Matthew's and Mark's statements, nor is there anything about the time being fulfilled. What could this possibly mean? How can Matthew and Mark tell us Jesus went into Galilee proclaiming the arrival of the kingdom and announcing that He was the Messiah, and Luke completely ignore this very important point? If we were to say that the Gospels were written under the prophetic model, we would have a very difficult time answering this question. For under the prophetic model this would mean that the vision God showed Matthew and Mark about Jesus' entry into Galilee is inconsistent with what was shown Luke.

However, under the Lucan model, we can allow the gospel writers latitude to work with their research materials as individual authors. As we examine their three summary statements we are confident that they are not based on inconsistent visions concerning the opening of Jesus' work in Galilee. We know that under the Lucan model Luke is using his brush to emphasize highlights of Jesus' portrait that are his own.

We can see Luke's highlights in the portrait at this point if we take Luke 4:14-30 as a unit. First, there is no proclamation by Jesus that the time is fulfilled, nor that the kingdom has arrived. Then Luke reports Jesus' visit to Nazareth. This gives us an entirely different opening to the Galilean ministry from that of Matthew and Mark. By now we are accustomed to asking that all-important question, What is Luke telling us?

We will follow the opening event of this visit to Jesus' hometown synagogue. "And he came to Nazareth, where he had been brought up; and went to the synagogue, as his custom was, on the sabbath day. And he stood up to read; and there was given him the book of the prophet Isaiah. He opened the book and found the place where it was written, 'The Spirit of the Lord is upon me, because he has anointed me to preach good news to the poor. He has sent me to proclaim release to the captives and recovering of sight to the blind, to set at liberty those who are oppressed, to proclaim the acceptable year of the Lord.' " Luke 4:16-19.

Everyone in the synagogue recognized this passage from Isaiah as a Messianic passage. Luke tells us that when Jesus finished reading, He rolled up the scroll, gave it back to the attendant, and stepped to the speaker's chair on the rostrum. When He had taken this position everyone knew He was going to deliver a sermon on the passage He just read. His opening words sent a shock wave through the congregation, "Today this scripture has been fulfilled in your hearing." Verse 21.

What has Luke accomplished as an author? He has presented

Jesus to his readers as the Messiah, as the fulfillment of Isaiah's prohecy. But more than this, by using the reading from the Isaiah scroll, Luke has outlined Jesus' whole ministry. Therefore, that which Jesus read from the Isaiah scroll becomes programmatic, i.e., the program of ministry that Jesus is going to follow.

In addition to all of this, the reading of Isaiah's prophecy becomes Luke's proclamation about the kingdom. But how different it is from Matthew's and Mark's. Whereas Matthew and Mark proclaim the kingdom as being present, to Luke its presence is of secondary importance. Luke does not proclaim that the kingdom is present until Jesus sends out the seventy disciples. Then He tells them that part of their message is to proclaim, "The kingdom of God is *ēggiken* [present]." See Luke 10:9. This is the first time Luke ties this word to the kingdom, while Matthew and Mark use the word in their introductory statement on the Galilean ministry.

Following the report on the mission of the seventy, Luke records another affirmation by Jesus that the kingdom is present, "But if it is by the finger of God that I cast out demons, then the kingdom of God has come upon you." Luke 11:20.

Why did Luke wait so long before he affirms the fact that Jesus proclaimed the kingdom as present? Using the passage read from the Isaiah scroll as a program of ministry, Luke develops the nature of the kingdom. Therefore, his readers, especially Theophilus, are lead to understand what the kingdom of Jesus is all about before they are informed that the kingdom is already present. If you will recall, this is just the reverse from Matthew, who proclaims the kingdom as present first and then explains its nature in the Sermon on the Mount. Obviously the nature of the audience to whom each writer is addressing his Gospel calls for this difference.

To summarize: The Lucan model of inspiration has helped us to see how three individual authors have guided us into the Galilean ministry of Jesus. All three present Jesus as the Messiah, the King. But each with varying touches of his brush brings out different highlights. After Jesus proclaimed the kingdom as being present, Matthew opens our understanding concerning the kingdom, its King, and the ethics of the citizens of the kingdom by presenting the Sermon on the Mount. In Mark, Jesus proclaims the presence of the kingdom and then demonstrates the truth of this fact by an exorcism. Although Luke does not make a proclamation on the presence of the kingdom at the beginning of the Galilean ministry, he introduces his readers to the kingdom nonetheless. The passage from the Isaiah scroll becomes the blueprint for Jesus' ministry. Because the major thrust of this prophecy is release, we are to understand, as far as the Gospel of Luke is concerned, that the kingdom of Jesus brings release from the control of the kingdom of Satan.

This has been a brief look at how the gospel writers worked as authors. However, because of the nature of Jesus and His mission, they say something theologically as well. We will examine their theological contributions next.

References

1. Ellen G. White, *The Desire of Ages* (Mountain View, Calif: Pacific Press Publishing Association, 1940), p. 299.
2. H. E. Dana and Fulius R. Mantey, *A Manual Grammar of the Greek New Testament* (New York: Macmillan Company, 1966), p. 202.

Gospel Writers as Theologians—Part I

It is difficult at times, if not impossible, to distinguish between a gospel writer as a literary author and as a theologian. The passages we examined in the previous chapter were used to illustrate our gospel writers as authors. These very same passages might be examined for their theological contributions. The Sermon on the Mount, the healing of the demoniac, and the reading of the Isaiah scroll have something to say theologically about the kingdom and its King. The individuality of each writer is seen in the choice of material to express his understanding of Jesus' teaching about the kingdom and Jesus' kingship.

As we study the contributions of the gospel writers as theologians, we shall concentrate on Luke. We have seen that Luke begins Jesus' Galilean ministry with His visit to Nazareth. In dealing with this visit, Luke introduces three important elements: (1) Jesus' relationship with the Sabbath (Luke 4:16), (2) the reading of the Isaiah scroll (Luke 4:17-20), and (3) Jesus' sermon that enrages the people to the point where they try to kill Him (Luke 4:21-30). For the moment, we are concerned with the content of the Isaiah scroll.

Luke gives this passage as a virtual quotation of Isaiah 61:1, 2 with echoes of 58:6. He records: "The Spirit of the Lord is upon me, because he has anointed me to preach good news to the poor. He has sent me to proclaim release to the captives and recovering of sight to the blind, to set at liberty those who are oppressed, to proclaim the acceptable year of the Lord." Luke 4:18, 19.

By concluding the reading of this passage with the words, "Today this scripture has been fulfilled in your hearing" (verse 21), all present understood that Jesus was claiming to be the individual spoken of by Isaiah. Because this passage was generally accepted as a Messianic passage, they realized Jesus was claiming His Messiahship.

This Messianic passage states three things about the Messiah: (1) He is chosen ("anointed") by God for a special mission, and this choice is evidenced by the infilling of the Holy Spirit, (2) His mission is to preach good news to the poor, and (3) the good news is made up of four parts: (a) "release to the captives," (b) "recovering of sight to the blind," (c) "liberty" for "those who are oppressed," and (d) "the acceptable year of the Lord."

It becomes clear at once that the central message and mission of the Messiah is that of release. The four parts of the "good news" makes this apparent. "Release to the captives" and "liberty" for "those who are oppressed" speak clearly about the release the Messiah was to bring. But the two remaining parts of the Messiah's mission also deal with release. "Recovering of sight to the blind" speaks of release from the kingdom of darkness, and "the acceptable year of the Lord" is a reference to the jubilee year—a year when slaves were freed and debts were canceled—certainly an experience of release. Therefore, according to Isaiah's prophecy, the mission and message of the Messiah would be that of release.

By choosing to begin Jesus' ministry with the reading of the Isaiah scroll, Luke is introducing a theological motif that he develops in his own way throughout his Gospel. The reader of Luke should become aware of this, as well as other motifs, and watch for them as he reads through Luke's Gospel. Only as one becomes sensitive to their presence will he be able to grasp what is being said about Jesus.

Lucan scholars are generally agreed that the Isaiah passage was introduced by Luke to announce Jesus' program of ministry.[1] With release being the central theme of this passage, the reader must ever keep before him the fact that Luke is portraying Jesus as the Divine Deliverer. Perhaps this can be best portrayed by examining the events following His visit to Nazareth.

To the casual reader, Luke would appear to be following essentially Mark's order of events. When we line these events up side by side, they appear as follows:

Mark	Luke
Call of first disciples (1:16-20)	
	Visit to Nazareth (4:16-30)
Demoniac at Capernaum (1:21-28)	Demoniac at Capernaum (4:31-37)
Healing many people (1:29-34)	Healing many people (4:38-41)
A preaching tour (1:35-39)	A preaching tour (4:42-44)
	Call of first disciples (5:1-11)
Cleansing of leper (1:40-45)	Cleansing of leper (5:12-16)
Healing of paralytic (2:1-12)	Healing of paralytic (5:17-26)
Call of Levi (2:13-17)	Call of Levi (5:27-32)
Question on fasting (2:18-22)	Question on fasting (5:33-39)
Plucking grain on Sabbath (2:23-28)	Plucking grain on Sabbath (6:1-5)
Man with withered hand (3:1-6)	Man with withered hand (6:6-11)

It might be mentioned at this point that Matthew has an entirely different sequence of events following the Sermon on the Mount. As we have come to suspect, there is a reason for this. We will discover this reason later on.

Coming back to the sequence of events in Mark and Luke, it appears that the only difference is the location of the call of the first disciples and the insertion of the visit to Nazareth at the beginning of the Lucan sequence. But the appearance of similarity is deceptive. First, when Mark and Luke are closely examined, it will be seen that there are many changes in the details of these events. Second, the relocation of the call to discipleship has profound meaning for Luke's portrait of Jesus. Third, the reading of the Isaiah scroll, i.e., the theme of release that is found in this prophecy, places all of these events that follow in Luke in an entirely different context from that of Mark, even though the events may be the same.

What we must understand is that we cannot read the cleansing of the leper in Luke, for example, in the same manner we read it in Mark. Why? Because in Luke the cleansing of the leper must be understood in the context of release, which is the motif established by the Isaiah prophecy. In Mark the cleansing of the leper must be understood in the context of Jesus' statement in the introduction to the Galilean ministry, "The time is fulfilled, the kingdom of God is at hand [is present]; repent, and believe in the gospel." Mark 1:15. That is to say, the cleansing of the leper in Mark is to be seen as a verification of Jesus' statement that the kingdom of God is here.

So we see the gospel writers, under the Lucan model, using the very same material to bring out different highlights in their portrait of Jesus.

In turning our attention to Luke, we discover that the events following Jesus' visit to Nazareth fall into three distinct groups. Each event within its own group contributes to what Luke is saying about Jesus. We will examine each group separately.

The first group contains the following events: (1) the healing of the demoniac at Capernaum (Luke 4:31-37), (2) the healing of many people (verses 38-41), (3) and the report of a preaching tour (verses 42-44). Upon reading these passages, it becomes clear that the common element is Jesus' confrontation with demonic powers. Let us follow the sequence of events.

After leaving Nazareth, Jesus entered Capernaum. Luke 4:31-37. Here, on Sabbath, He went to the synagogue and taught the people. A demon-possessed man broke up the service and confronted Jesus, whereupon Jesus exorcised him. The people responded, "What is this word? For with authority and power he commands the unclean spirits, and they come out." Verse 36. The story is virtually the same as it appears in Mark. But remember, Luke's message is different from the one set forth by Mark.

Here the healing of the demoniac is set into the Lucan milieu—release. Bear this in mind: Isaiah prophesied that the Messiah would "proclaim release to the captives." Verse 18. Jesus said to the evil spirit possessing this man, " 'Be silent, and come out of him!' And when the demon had thrown him down in the midst, he came out of him, having done him no harm." Verse 35.

"Release to the captives"! Luke saw a different use for the story of the demoniac at Capernaum than Mark saw, even though he no doubt received the story from Mark. The close parallel between Mark's account and Luke's account seems to testify that Luke took careful notes as Mark, the *hupēretēs,* repeated the story. But whereas Mark used this miracle to show that the kingdom had indeed arrived, Luke used it to show how Jesus was a fulfillment of Isaiah's prophecy. "Today this scripture has been fulfilled in your hearing." Verse 21.

The healing of the demoniac shows that Jesus' ministry will bring release to the captives of Satan. This is the theme of the first group of events that follow Jesus' visit to Nazareth.

The next event in this first group follows the service in the synagogue. Here is how Luke records it, "And he arose and left the synagogue, and entered Simon's house. Now Simon's mother-in-law was ill with a high fever, and they besought him for her. And he stood over her and rebuked the fever, and it left her; and immediately she rose and served them." Luke 4:38, 39.

I would like to treat this passage in detail under another heading; therefore, I will simply point the reader's attention to how Jesus healed Peter's mother-in-law. He "rebuked the fever." He spoke to the fever as though it possessed intelligence. There is good reason to believe that the Jews understood a high fever to be caused by a fever demon.[2] Using this popular belief as a teaching device, Luke presented Jesus as healing Peter's mother-in-law by bringing release from the captivity of Satan, the fever demon. This healing is told in quite a different way by Matthew and Mark. But, as I have already remarked, we shall examine all of this in greater detail later.

Luke continues by telling us that when the sun went down on that Sabbath, "all those who had any that were sick with various diseases brought them to him; and he laid his hands on every one of them and healed them." Verse 40. Among those brought for healing were many who were demon possessed. It is concerning these, among all who were healed that night, that Luke gives the greatest detail: "And demons also came out of many, crying, 'You are the Son of God!' But he rebuked them, and would not allow them to speak, because they knew that he was the Christ." Verse 41. Unquestionably the emphasis in this second event of the first group is on release from Satan's power. The healing of Peter's mother-in-law and the many exorcisms that followed after sunset strengthen Luke's portrait of Jesus as a Bringer of release.

The final event in this first group contains a statement by Jesus that ties what precedes it into a meaningful package. According to the story, Jesus went off alone into the wilderness. When the crowds found Him, they urged Him to stay with them and not to go anywhere else. It is Jesus' reply that we are interested in. Notice the differences when we compare it with Mark, the only other gospel writer to record it.

Mark	Luke
And he said to them, "Let us go on to the next towns, that I may preach there also; for that is why I came out." And he went throughout all Galilee, preaching in their synagogues and casting out demons (1:38, 39).	But he said to them, "I must preach the good news of the kingdom of God to the other cities also; for I was sent for this purpose." And he was preaching in the synagogues of Judea (4:43, 44).

First we notice that Mark said Jesus went into synagogues to preach and He cast out demons. Mark was continuing the theme he established at the beginning. As Jesus made His circuit from synagogue to synagogue, His message was that the kingdom of God had arrived. The casting out of demons was evidence of this, just as it was in the synagogue at Capernaum.

In Luke there is no further mention of exorcisms. Rather, Jesus said, "I must preach the good news of the kingdom of God." On the basis of Luke's context, as the preceding events have shown us, what is the good news of the kingdom? It is release to the captives of Satan.

What have we seen so far? We have seen Luke working as a theologian. He used his material to make a theological statement about Jesus and the kingdom. But we must not stop here. Luke wishes us to see additional details in his portrait of Jesus.

The second group of events that show how the Isaiah prophecy is fulfilled by Jesus begins with the call of the first disciples. Luke 5:1-11. This is followed by the cleansing of a leper (verses 12-16), the healing of a paralytic (verses 17-26), and the call of Levi (verses 27-32).

The reader has already been alerted to the fact that Luke relocates the call of the first disciples. He is also aware that the prophetic model cannot explain why Matthew and Mark have this call right at the beginning of Jesus' ministry, whereas Luke has it at this point. However, when working with the Lucan model of inspiration, logical answers are forthcoming. The reasons for the change in position of this event will be presented later. Right now we want to see how the call to discipleship fits into Luke's motif of release.

In connection with the call to discipleship in Luke's Gospel, we find a miracle performed by Jesus. After preaching from Simon's boat, Jesus ordered the fishermen out into the lake for a catch of fish. Knowing that such an occurrence was highly unlikely, Simon expressed his reluctance to comply with Jesus' command. And yet, against his better judgment, he indicated a willingness to comply with Jesus' instruction. At Jesus' word, the nets were lowered. To Simon's utter amazement, a school of fish was encircled, so large that the nets began to break. Even with the help of Simon's partners and their boat, the catch was so big that both boats were in danger of being swamped.

Completely overwhelmed by what he saw, Simon cast himself at Jesus' feet and exclaimed, " 'Depart from me, for I am a sinful man, O Lord.' " Verse 8. Many comentators deal with the large catch of fish. They tell us how this successful fishing endeavor, which Simon saw as fraught with formidable odds, was an assurance that, if the disciples responded to Jesus' invitation, they would have similar success as fishers of men.[3] This explanation of the passage may be true, but it is not the primary truth that Luke wanted his readers to see. The climax of this event was Peter's confession of his sinfulness, which came from the realization that he stood in the presence of One who was more than man. As Luke said, "For he was astonished, and all that were with him, at the catch of fish which they had taken." Verse 9. The word *astonished (thambos)* could more effectively be translated "awe struck."

Jesus replied, "Do not be afraid; henceforth you will be catching men." Verse 10. Here is what Luke wanted his readers to see. A sinful man, admitting his sinfulness, and a forgiving Saviour telling him not to fear, that on the basis of his confession he is accepted and invited to become a co-worker with the Saviour. It is the problem of sin that Luke is after, and the release from sin that only Jesus can bring.

Observe how this fits into Luke's motif of release and why Luke moved the call to discipleship to this point in his narrative. But now notice how this is integrated with what follows.

Simon's confession introduces the issue of sin. Jesus' calling of Peter, James, and John to discipleship showed that He was here to bring release from the power of sin. The reader might legitimately ask: How is this release to be accomplished? The answer comes in the next event recorded by Luke—the cleansing of the leper. If you will recall, in Mark's sequence, the cleansing of the leper follows the report of a preaching tour. The issue of sin has not been introduced. Therefore, the cleansing of the leper in Mark is merely evidence added to the healing of demoniacs that the kingdom of God is present.

The rearrangement of the call of the first disciples, with Simon's confession of his sinfulness, introduces an element that is not in Mark—the element of sin. Now the cleansing of the leper comes to bear on this new element. Luke 5:12-16. What is the result? A further development of Luke's motif of release.

First of all, we know that in the Jewish mind leprosy was a symbol of sin. It was commonly called "the stroke of God," or "the touch of the finger of God." Next we need to take note of how Jesus and this leper met. Luke begins this story by saying, "While

he was in one of the cities, there came a man full of leprosy."
Verse 12. This statement needs further examination. First, neither
Matthew nor Mark say the man was "full of leprosy." Matthew
says, "When he came down from the mountain, great crowds followed him; and behold, a leper came to him and knelt before
him." Matthew 8:1, 2. Mark reports, "And a leper came to him
beseeching him, and kneeling said to him." Mark 1:40. Why does
Luke report him to be a man "full of leprosy?" This simple addition helps him with the details of Jesus' portrait.

Before we see how this is so, we need to ask these questions:
What is this leper doing in a city? Are not lepers banned from
cities, from places of population? Why did he not cry for help
from a distance as did other lepers (cf. Luke 17:12)? What can
Luke possibly be telling us by adding the information that this
man was full of leprosy and that he found Jesus in the city?

The statement that he was full of leprosy may be clarified by
examining the law that deals with such cases. This, in turn, will
explain why the leper freely mixed with people in the city. Leviti-
cus 13:12, 13 says, "And if the leprosy breaks out in the skin, so
that the leprosy covers all the skin of the diseased person from
head to foot, so far as the priest can see, then the priest shall make
an examination, and if the leprosy has covered all his body, he
shall pronounce him clean of the disease; it has all turned white,
and he is clean."

The description of leprosy given here would seem to fit the man
that Luke is describing. "Full of leprosy" certainly fits "from
head to foot." When the disease has spread to this extent, the man
is clean. Does this mean the man no longer has the disease? No,
he is "full" of the disease. What this text does seem to say is that
it was believed that the disease was no longer contagious. It appears probable that the man in Luke's Gospel was very close to
death. The disease had covered his whole body. But it was no
longer considered communicable. This explains why he was
permitted in the city and why he no longer had to warn people of
his approach. The man was allowed to return to his family and die
at home.

But how important these added details are. Luke has introduced the issue of sin through Simon's confession. He adds the

information that this man was "full of leprosy," and we know that leprosy was thought of as a symbol of sin. Because this unfortunate man could freely move about in the city would seem to indicate the disease had progressed to the point where it was no longer contagious, but was now terminal. What an accurate representation of the human race. Luke's description of the leper represents us.

This man came to Jesus for help. "Lord," he said, "if you will, you can make me clean." Luke 5:12. Without a moment's hesitation Jesus reached out His hand and touched the leper, saying, "I will, be clean." Verse 13. How will God deal with the sin issue that is introduced by Simon's confession? The answer is found in the "touch" and in the authority that lies in Jesus. God will deal with sin by coming into personal contact with it, i.e., the "touch" in the story of the leper. But what about the authority? Does Jesus possess the authority to bring release from sin?

The next event deals with the healing of a paralytic. Verses 17-26. When this man was lowered through the roof into Jesus' presence, Jesus said, "Man, your sins are forgiven you." Verse 20. The reaction of Jesus' critics was swift, "Who is this that speaks blasphemies? Who can forgive sins but God only?" Verse 21. Do you see now what Luke has accomplished by moving the call to discipleship into its present position?

Well, does Jesus have the authority to release men from sin? The question of Jesus' antagonists sets the stage for what followed. Jesus replied, " 'Why do you question in your hearts? Which is easier, to say, "Your sins are forgiven you," or to say, "Rise and walk?" But that you may know that the Son of man has authority on earth to forgive sins'—he said to the man who was paralyzed—'I say to you, rise, take up your bed and go home.' And immediately he rose before them, and took up that on which he lay, and went home, glorifying God." Verses 22-25.

When the paralytic picked up his bed and walked out of the house, the question was forever settled. Jesus did possess the authority to release men from the power of sin. By introducing Simon's confession of his sinfulness at the exact point where he does, Luke uses the material found in Mark for a purpose that is uniquely his. This is a typical example of a gospel writer functioning as a theologian under the Lucan model of inspiration.

Luke is not finished with his motif of release from the power of sin. The call of the first disciples makes it clear that when Jesus extended release from sin, He also extended an invitation to enter His kingdom and to become co-workers with Him. The call of Levi Matthew complements the call of Simon and his partners, as well as concludes Luke's motif on release from sin.

By extending an invitation to Matthew, the tax collector, to join Him in His labors, Jesus showed the extent to which the kingdom was to be offered and release from sin was to be given. It was a well-known fact that any Jew who accepted the job of collecting taxes for the Roman oppressor was despised by his people and considered a traitor. By calling Matthew, the lesson is taught that the kingdom is open to the very "dregs" of society, provided they are willing to accept Jesus' invitation.

There is much in this story that must be understood, if its concluding lines are to have any meaning for us. First, those who were attending the feast make the story more dramatic. Luke tells us "there was a large company of tax collectors and others sitting at table with them [Jesus and His disciples]." Verse 29. We know who the tax collectors were, but is there any way of identifying the "others"? The Greek word helps us. Here is is *allōn,* which means others of the same kind. Luke does not specify who they were; rather, he allows his readers to use their imagination. The "others" would be those who cared little about what the religious leaders thought of them. They chose their company to their own liking, and they chose to associate with tax collectors. A pious Jew, disdaining to associate with this class of people, would shake his head and say, "Birds of a feather flock together." When the scribes and Pharisees found fault with Jesus and His disciples, they asked, "Why do you eat and drink with tax collectors and sinners?" Verse 30. One would suppose that the "sinners" indentified here would be the "others" in verse 29 who associated with the tax collectors. However, the laws of Greek grammar show that the scribes and Pharisees made no distinction between the assembled guests. They lumped together everyone who had been invited to the feast. Everyone there was a tax collector and a sinner so far as the religious leaders were concerned.

Why were the scribes and Pharisees so upset by this? The reason is that Jesus, who was recognized by the common people as one of the leading religious teachers of that time, was ignoring the cermonial purity regulations that governed Jewish society. Eating at the table of such a person as Matthew rendered Jesus and His disciples ceremonially impure. This in turn disqualified them from carrying out certain religious obligations required of every Jew. If Jesus was allowed to continue such behavior unchecked, pious Jews everywhere were in danger of being influenced by what they considered to be His bad example. The whole system of ritual purity and impurity was in danger of being thrown into confusion. This was the cause of their concern.

The second point that must be understood is what transpired between Jesus and the tax collectors and "others." In the culture of the Middle East, accepting the hospitality of a person was more than just a social gesture. It indicated a mutual obligation of one to the other. But this author believes that in the case in question, the implications of this feast far surpassed human obligations. Table fellowship also carried implications when one dined at a feast prepared in honor of a god. To eat at a table spread in honor of a god implied a willingness on the part of the participants to enter into a covenant relationship with the god. It was this very point that upset the apostle Paul when he learned what some Christians in Corinth were doing. As a result, he wrote three chapters of counsel (1 Corinthians 8-10).

Thus, for example, we find the apostle writing to them, "For if any one sees you, a man of knowledge, at table in an idol's temple, might he not be encouraged, if his conscience is weak, to eat food offered to idols?" 1 Corinthians 8:10. At the conclusion of his discourse on this topic Paul said, "What do I imply then? That food offered to idols is anything, or that an idol is anything? No, I imply that what pagans sacrifice they offer to demons and not to God. I do not want you to be partners with demons. You cannot drink the cup of the Lord and the cup of demons. You cannot partake of the table of the Lord and the table of demons. Shall we provoke the Lord to jealousy? Are we stronger than he?" 1 Corinthians 10:19-22.

What has all this to do with Matthew's feast? Simply this. In the event that preceded Matthew's feast, Jesus healed a paralytic. This miracle centered in the question whether Jesus had authority to forgive sins. Remember, Jesus said to the man, "Your sins are forgiven you." Luke 5:20. The religious leaders responded by saying, "Who is this that speaks blasphemies? Who can forgive sins but God only?" Verse 21. The question posed by the religious authorities set the stage for the miracle. By healing the paralytic, Jesus not ony showed He had authority to forgive sins, but by the very fact He did such a thing testified that He was indeed God.

Now we need to notice a very small addition that Luke makes in this story that is not found in Matthew's and Mark's accounts. In verse 29 we are told that Matthew made this great feast for Jesus, in which the latter was the Guest of honor. This minor addition gives a whole new complexion to this feast in Luke. Jesus had just proven Himself to be God; now He is depicted at a feast given in His honor, surrounded by tax collectors and sinners. What is Luke telling us by painting such a picture? Jesus was opening up the gates to the kingdom and inviting the publicans and sinners to come in. Eating together at this banquet indicated that Jesus was inviting these outcasts of society into the covenant relationship with Him. This is confirmed by Jesus' closing words directed to the Jewish religious leaders, "Those who are well have no need of a physician, but those who are sick; I have not come to call the righteous, but sinners to repentance." Verses 31, 32.

By relocating the call of the first disicples, Luke was able to introduce the issue of sin. By selecting which miracles follow, by changing little things here and there throughout, he was able to show how Jesus brings release from sin. So we see a second way in which Jesus fulfilled the Isaiah prophecy which He read in the synagogue at Nazareth.

The third group of events deals with the release from cultic traditions and can be seen in the question about fasting (Luke 5:33-39), plucking grain on the Sabbath (Luke 6:1-5), and healing the man with the withered hand on the Sabbath (Luke 6:6-11).

Jesus was criticized for not teaching His disciples to fast. The Pharisees and their disciples fasted every Monday and Thursday.[4]

From the criticism that was leveled at Jesus, we can assume that John the Baptist's disciples must have followed a similar practice. "And they said to him, 'The disciples of John fast often and offer prayers, and so do the disciples of the Pharisees, but yours eat and drink.' " Luke 5:33. The number of times a person fasted was believed to be a sign of a person's piety. It was considered meritorious and surely something that a pious Jew would not neglect. Jesus' response to this charge showed that He did not reject the idea of fasting; rather, He revealed that fasting must be properly motivated.

He then told His critics two little parables, "No one tears a piece from a new garment and puts it upon an old garment; if he does, he will tear the new, and the piece from the new will not match the old. And no one puts new wine into old wineskins; if he does, the new wine will burst the skins and it will be spilled, and the skins will be destroyed. But new wine must be put into fresh wineskins." Verses 36-38. There is general agreement among commentators that the new garment and the new wine that Jesus speaks of represents Christianity.[5] The old, tattered garment and old wineskins represent Judaism. These two little parables make it clear that Jesus knew it would be impossible to combine the old and the new. He knew He could not impose the gospel of release that He preached upon the structure of Judaism. The old structure could not bear the weight of the new. It would collapse, and both Judaism and Christianity would suffer.

Therefore, Jesus called those who would respond into a new relationship with Him: "New wine must be put into fresh wineskins." His gospel contained the power not only to bring release from Satan's power and from sin, but also to release from the old religious system of meritorious works. But Jesus knew that the old system of human works was very satisfying and that many would not accept the new. Luke closes these two parables with a saying that neither Matthew nor Mark contains. There has been a great deal of discussion as to where it originated. However, there is no reason to reject it as being spoken by Jesus, for He was well aware of the hostility against Him and His gospel. Therefore, Jesus concluded with, "No one after drinking old wine desires new; for he says, 'The old is good.' " Verse 39.

The issue of fasting is immediately followed by two Sabbath events. Many point to these events and claim they have found evidence for the transfer of the Sabbath from the seventh day to the first day of he week. However, the careful reader will see that these Sabbath events have nothing to do with a change in the day of worship; rather they have to do with proper Sabbath observance.

The disciples' plucking of the grain on the Sabbath and the healing of the man with the withered hand both teach the same truth, i.e., the humanitarian nature of God's holy rest day. Just before Jesus restored the cripple's withered hand in the synagog, He asked those who wished to bring an accusation against Him, "Is it lawful on the sabbath to do good or to do harm, to save life or to destroy it?" Luke 6:9.

The Jews, by man-made restrictions, had made the Sabbath a burden that was heavy to bear. However, to this day, many Jews insist that the extra restrictions that were placed upon the Sabbath did not make it burdensome to the people, but a delight.[6] Jesus evidently thought otherwise. He repeatedly disregarded these restrictions and taught, by His example, a different standard of Sabbath observance.

By starting the ministry of Jesus with the reading of the Isaiah scroll, Luke's gospel establishes the motif of release. The material that follows this event in Christ's life should be read and understood within the context of this theme—even the story about fasting and the question of how the Sabbath is to be observed. By so doing, we can see that Jesus' intention was not to abolish fasting and the Sabbath, but to free these practices from human encroachment—from human restrictions that stripped them of their true meaning and value.

Although Luke followed Mark's order rather closely, we can see that by introducing Jesus' ministry with the reading of the Isaiah scroll, he sets this material within his own thematic milieu. This is further strengthened by the relocation of the call of the first disciples and smaller changes and additions throughout. Therefore, we can say that although Luke's material at this point is very close to Mark's, it is Luke's nonetheless.

The motif of release that Luke develops is an excellent example of a gospel writer as a theologian. We have an excellent example of this in Matthew as well. Therefore, before we leave this general topic, we must see what Matthew does and how he accomplishes his purpose in an entirely different way.

References

1. Cf. G. B. Caird, *The Gospel of St. Luke* (Baltimore: Penguin Books, 1963), p. 86; John Martin Creed, *The Gospel According to St. Luke* (London: Macmillan & Co., Ltd., 1960), p. 66; Frederick W. Danker, *Luke* (Philadelphia: Fortress Press, 1976), p. 74; Burton Scott Easton, *The Gospel According to St. Luke: A Critical and Exegetical Commentary* (Edinburgh: T & T Clark, 1926), p. 50; Norval Geldenhuys, *Commentary on the Gospel of Luke* (Grand Rapids, Mich.: William B. Eerdmans Publishing Company, 1954), p. 170; William Manson, *The Gospel of Luke* (New York: Richard R. Smith, Inc., 1930), p. 41; I. Howard Marshall, *The Gospel of Luke: A Commentary on the Greek Text* (Grand Rapids, Mich.: William B. Eerdmans Publishing Company, 1978), pp. 177, 178; C. G. Montefiore, *The Synoptic Gospels* (London: Macmillan and Company, Ltd., 1909), vol. 2, p. 873.

2. W. O. E. Oesterly, *The Jews and Judaism During the Greek Period: The Background of Christianity* (London: Society for Promoting Christian Knowledge, 1941), pp. 289, 290; Frederick W. Danker, *Jesus and the New Age According to St. Luke: A Commentary on the Third Gospel* (St. Louis: Clayton Publishing House, 1972), pp. 62, 91; Joseph Dillersberger, *The Gospel of St. Luke* (Westminster, Md.: Newman Press, 1958), p. 190; John Drury, *Luke* (New York: Macmillan Publishing Co., Inc., 1973), p. 59. The activity of demons played a major role in Jewish folklore, as it did in Gentile folklore. At that period many home remedies for physical ills revolved around superstitions rooted in this folklore. Although the Jews believed that many physical problems were caused by demons, we must remember that Luke is writing to Theophilus, a man with a Gentile background. Hence the healing Peter's mother-in-law by speaking to a supposed "fever demon" would certainly be meaningful to Theophilus and would demonstrate to him Jesus' power over the demon world. To those Jews who superstitiously believed in a "fever demon," the authority of Jesus would be evident. When Jesus healed this woman, He may have very well seized or touched her hand as reported by Matthew and Mark, and at the same time He may have spoken, as reported by Luke. Because of the superstition commonly held among the Gentiles and among many Jews, Luke chose to report only the verbal command of Jesus. Thus making it possible for this healing to fit into the motif of release from Satan's power that he was developing at this point.

3. William F. Arndt, *The Gospel According to St. Luke* (St. Louis: Concordia Publishing House, 1956), p. 155; Creed, p. 73; Drury, p. 62; Montefiore, p. 879.

4. Cf. Luke 18:12; George Foot Moore, *Judaism in the First Centuries of the Christian Era: The Age of the Tannaim* (Cambridge: Harvard University Press, 1932), vol. 2, p. 260.

5. The following two sources disagree. Alestair Kee, "The Old Coat and the New Wine," *Novum Testamentum,* XII (January 1970): 13-21; Paul Trudinger, "The Word on the Generation Gap: Reflections on a Gospel Metaphor," *Biblical Theology Bulletin,* V (October 1975): 311-315. Also see my article where I point

out the weaknesses of Kee's and Trudinger's positions as far as Luke is concerned, "Luke 5:33-6:11: Release From Cultic Tradition," *Andrews University Seminary Studies,* 20 (Summer 1982): 127-132.

6. A. Cohen, *Everyman's Talmud* (New York: E. P. Dutton & Co., Inc., 1949), p. 155.

Gospel Writers as Theologians—Part II

In the last chapter, we saw how Luke, as a theologian, worked with the material that he had gathered. He painted a picture of Jesus as the Bringer of release—release from the captivity of Satan, release from sin, and release from cultic traditions. We also saw that the majority of Luke's material throughout that section is very similar to Mark's Gospel. Yet, despite this similarity, we found Lucan touches here and there. As a result this material became uniquely his own. He accomplished this feat by introducing Jesus' ministry with a prophecy from Isaiah. This prohecy then became the blueprint for Jesus' work as Deliverer. Luke further stamped this "Marcan material" as his by relocating the call of the first disciples and making small alterations that advanced the motif of "release."

By comparing the gospel accounts of Luke and Mark, we also saw that Mark adheres to his own portrait of Jesus. He set the tone for Jesus' ministry with the introductory statement, "Jesus came into Galilee . . . saying, 'The time is fulfilled, and the kingdom of God is at hand [is present].' " Mark 1:14, 15. The very same miracles used by Luke to develop the motif of release are used by Mark (without the Lucan adjustments) to show that the kingdom of God indeed had arrived. Thus we saw Mark working as a theologian developing his understanding of Jesus. Now, what about Matthew?

As we have already seen, Matthew's account follows Jesus' statement concerning the presence of the kingdom with the Sermon on the Mount. We have also seen that this sermon functions as a statement concerning the nature of the kingdom, the nature of its King, and what is expected of those who are its citizens. Prior to this sermon Matthew established the fact that Jesus is the King of Israel. Following this sermon, he established a second point about Jesus. It is this second point that we wish to develop in this chapter.

If we compare Matthew with the other two synoptics we will see an interesting rearrangement of events. We will begin with the opening events of the Galilean ministry.

Matthew	Mark	Luke
Sermon on the Mount (5-7)		Visit to Nazareth (4:16-30)
Cleansing of leper (8:1-4)	Healing demoniac (1:21-28)	Healing demoniac (4:31-37)
Healing centurion's servant (8:5-13)	Healing many people (1:29-34)	Healing many people (4:38-41)
Healing many people (8:14-17)	Preaching tour (1:35-39)	Preaching tour (4:42-44)
Would-be followers (8:18-22)		Call of first disciples (5:1-11)
Calming storm (8:23-27)	Cleansing leper (1:40-45)	Cleansing leper (5:12-16)
Healing Gadarene demoniacs (8:28-34)		
Healing paralytic (9:1-8)	Healing paralytic (2:1-12)	Healing paralytic (5:17-26)

When these miracles are lined up side by side and analyzed it becomes clear that Matthew was not following Mark's sequence. Even though Luke's series appears to be close to Mark, we have learned that Luke has cast his material in a different context from Mark's. It becomes obvious that all three writers are working independently from each other as theologians. What is Matthew telling us by his sequence of events that follows the Sermon on the Mount?

Have you ever noticed as you have read through this section of

Matthew that each of the miracles he mentions, except one (we will take note of this one exception in the next chapter), is performed by the spoken word of Jesus? What is Matthew trying to tell us by so doing?

Matthew concluded the Sermon on the Mount with an observation as to how Jesus' words were received. These two concluding verses also serve as a means of transition to the second point that he established. They read as follows, "And when Jesus finished these sayings, the crowds were astonished at his teaching, for he taught them as one who had authority, and not as their scribes." Matthew 7:28, 29.

The reaction of the crowd was favorable. They were impressed with the authority *(eksousia)* with which Jesus spoke. His whole manner of delivery, the confidence He displayed in what He said, and the position of authority He assigned Himself in relation to what He taught was so different from the way the scribes taught that His hearers marveled.

Matthew capitalized on the impression that was made on the crowd by developing the idea of the authority of Jesus' word. What would this say to Matthew's readers? It is almost unanimously agreed that Matthew addressed his Gospel to his fellow Jews. What would they understand him to be saying by developing the authority of Jesus' word?

Immediately, there comes to mind the role assigned to God's word in the Old Testament. The word of God possessed authority. It was dynamic, creative energy. The very first chapter of the Bible introduces us to its creative power. "And God said, 'Let there be light'; and there was light." Genesis 1:3. "And God said, 'Let there be a firmament in the midst of the waters.' " Genesis 1:6, etc.

Looking back at the power of God's creative word, the psalmist said, "By the word of the Lord the heavens were made, and all their host by the breath of his mouth." "For he spoke, and it came to be; he commanded, and it stood forth." Psalm 33:6, 9. Speaking to Isaiah, God said, "So shall my word be that goes forth from my mouth; it shall not return to me empty, but it shall accomplish that which I purpose." Isaiah 55:11.

The Old Testament concept of the authority and dynamic

power of God's word is reflected in the New Testament, but, of course, here it is Jesus' word. "He reflects the glory of God and bears the very stamp of his nature, upholding the universe by his word of power." Hebrews 1:3. "For the word of God is living and active, sharper than any two-edged sword, piercing to the division of soul and spirit, of joint and marrow, and discerning the thoughts and intentions of the heart." Hebrews 4:12.

Matthew uses the Jewish concept of the power and authority of God's word to develop the second point he wished his readers to see about Jesus. Following his comment on the astonishment of the crowd that Jesus taught with authority, he collected together a series of events in which Jesus performed a miracle by the spoken word, thus demonstrating the power and energy of Jesus' word. In order to accomplish this, Matthew chose some of the very same miracles that Mark and Luke used to follow the event they selected to open the ministry of Jesus. But he also introduced other miracles that are scattered throughout the other synoptics. Thus Matthew developed his own sequence of events; and the power of Jesus' word to heal said something to Matthew's Jewish readers about the nature of Jesus. We will now take a look at these miracles.

The first event Matthew lists is the cleansing of the leper. Matthew 8:1-4. The leper came to Jesus and said, "Lord, if you will, you can make me clean." Verse 2. Jesus responded by stretching out His hand and touching him, saying, "I will; be clean." Verse 3. In Luke's sequence the "touch" of Jesus was the thing of importance. This is how God is to settle the sin issue. Here in Matthew, the spoken word of Jesus is the important act, "I will; be clean." Although Matthew records the fact that Jesus touched the man, it is the spoken command that brings the healing, "Be clean." Because of Matthew's emphasis on the authority of Jesus' word at the conclusion of the Sermon on the Mount, and the fact that we have a sequence of miracles resulting from Jesus' spoken word, it seems evident where Matthew wants us to place the emphasis in this miracle.

The story of the leper is followed by the healing of the centurion's servant. Matthew 8:5-13. As you know by looking at the listing of events, Luke does not have this miracle as early in his Gospel. As a matter of fact, if you read Luke's account of this miracle, you will find several significant differences. Mark does not record it at all.

The centurion came to Jesus and said, "Lord, my servant is lying paralyzed at home, in terrible distress." Verse 6. Whereupon Jesus offered to go to the centurion's home to heal the servant. The centurion replied, "Lord, I am not worthy to have you come under my roof; but only say the word, and my servant will be healed. For I am a man under authority, with soldiers under me; and I say to one, 'Go,' and he goes, and to another, 'Come,' and he comes, and to my slave, 'Do this,' and he does it." Verses 8, 9.

Obviously impressed with this demonstration of faith in His authority and power, Jesus said to the centurion, " 'Go; be it done for you as you have believed.' And the servant was healed at that very moment." Verse 13. Located in an entirely different cluster of incidents in Luke, this miracle is moved forward to its present location by Matthew because the centurion's servant was healed by the spoken word of Jesus.

The next event Matthew shares with Mark and Luke. It is the healing of Peter's mother-in-law and the miracles of healing Jesus performed after sunset, when the Sabbath was past. Verses 14-17. When we dealt with this occurrence earlier in connection with the gospel of Luke, I said we would examine it more closely later. At this point we shall notice two things concerning Matthew's account and hold further comment until later.

First of all, we need to notice that in both Mark and Luke the context of this event is the Sabbath. Jesus was in the synagogue at Capernaum and healed the demon-possessed man. When the services were over, He went to Simon's house, where He found his mother-in-law ill with a fever. In Matthew nothing is said about this day being the Sabbath. Because Matthew did not record the healing of the demoniac in the synagogue on the Sabbath, he removed the Sabbath context in connection with the healing of Peter's mother-in-law. This is supporting evidence that Jesus' miracles are not recorded in their chronological order. However, a remnant of the original context remained in Matthew, for he said, "That evening they brought to him many who were possessed with demons." Verse 16. The words "that evening" clearly reflect the original Sabbath context of the occurence and the gathering of the crowd after sunset.

The second thing we need to notice is that Matthew's report of the casting out of the evil spirits occurring that evening was written to fit into the motif he was developing, "and he cast out the spirits with a word." Verse 16. Matthew alone reported that the demons were exorcised "with a word" by Jesus. Here again we see a small alteration being made that changes an account shared by the other synoptic writers. The result is (1) the account now fits Matthew's motif of the authority of Jesus' spoken word, and (2) the small alteration becomes the unique contribution of Matthew.

Matthew then concluded this little story with a statement that again is unique to him: "This was to fulfil what was spoken by the prophet Isaiah, 'He took our infirmities and bore our diseases.' " Verse 17. Mark and Luke do not quote Isaiah at this point. Matthean scholars will hasten to point out that this is a characteristic of Matthew's style. He repeatedly quoted the Old Testament to show how Jesus fulfilled prophecy. By having compassion upon the demon possessed and those who were ill, by extending to them His healing power, Matthew saw Jesus as taking our infirmities and disease upon Himself.

However, this statement from Isaiah also gave Matthew the opportunity to show his readers another way Jesus shared in our infirmities. He moved into this sequence an event that Luke records at a much later time. "Now when Jesus saw great crowds around him, he gave orders to go over to the other side. And a scribe came up and said to him, 'Teacher, I will follow you wherever you go.' And Jesus said to him, 'Foxes have holes, and birds of the air have nests; but the Son of man has nowhere to lay his head.' Another of the disciples said to him, 'Lord, let me first go and bury my father.' But Jesus said to him, 'Follow me, and leave the dead to bury their own dead.' " Verses 18-22.

We have a very interesting situation with these verses. First, the opening line ties them to the miracle that follows in Matthew, i.e., the calming of the sea. Matthew begins these verses by saying that Jesus wished to "go over to the other side." This must be understood to refer to the Sea of Galilee. In Luke's report of these two would-be disciples there is no mention of the sea nor going over to the other side. Neither is there a connection with the miracle of calming the sea. It is set in an entirely different context with an entirely different ending. Again, it is clear that we have two writers using the same story for two different purposes, changing details to fit their purposes.

It may very well be that the story of these two would-be disciples was connected to the troubled crossing of Galilee, as Matthew's opening statement suggests. Matthew could have taken the sea crossing by itself, because, as we will see, it fits the motif he is developing. However, he saw a use for the two would-be disciples. By adding the quote from Isaiah to the conclusion of the mass healings after sunset, Matthew was able to show how Jesus identified with the woes of humanity. The two would-be disciples further Jesus' identity. He has nowhere to lay His head, and He forsook His filial attachments to become our Saviour. Although the two would-be disciples interrupt Matthew's main motif, he saw a truth important enough to insert here for the benefit of his readers.

Matthew now returns to the development of the motif of the power and authority of Jesus' word. Jesus and His disciples got into a boat and set sail for the other side of the lake. Verses 23-27. Caught by an unexpected storm, the disciples were in danger of drowning. When they woke the sleeping Saviour, they cried, "Save, Lord; we are perishing." Verse 25. Jesus not only rebuked the disciples for their lack of faith, but He rebuked the wind and the sea as well. "And there was a great calm." Verse 26. Those who witnessed the miracle were overwhelmed, for the wind and sea obeyed the spoken command of Jesus. He not only had authority over diseases and demons, He commanded nature as well, and nature obeyed His voice.

Arriving at their destination, the group was met by two fierce demoniacs. Verses 28-34. Knowing Jesus to be the Son of God, they pleaded with Him, "If you cast us out, send us away into the herd of swine." Verse 31. Jesus spoke a single word, "Go." Verse 32. At the spoken command, the demons fled their hosts and entered the swine.

Both Mark and Luke record the crossing of the sea and the healing of the Gadarene demoniacs (although they speak in terms of a single demoniac, not two). However, they do so later in their Gospels and they place it within a different context. It is interesting to note that all three synoptic writers keep the crossing of the lake and the healing together as a unit. Therefore, it is safe to assume that this is indeed the sequence in which the events recorded happened.

Upon returning to the other side of the lake, a paralytic was brought to Jesus while He was teaching in a house. Matthew 9:1-8. Luke used this miracle to show that Jesus does possess authority to bring release from sin. Matthew used it to climax the series of miracles that were performed by the spoken word. By His word He forgave this man's sins, and by His word the man rose and walked. The healing of this cripple established the fact that Jesus does possess power to forgive sins. This demonstration of authority to forgive sins climaxes what Matthew has been developing by showing the authority of Jesus' spoken word—He is God. This is the second point that Matthew wished to tell his readers about Jesus.

In summary: We have seen the three synoptic writers working as theologians. All three begin the ministry of Jesus with different events. Matthew used the Sermon on the Mount to show the nature of the kingdom and the nature of its King. Using the amazement of the crowd at the authority of Jesus' word, he built a motif that showed Jesus as God. A series of miracles, all performed by Jesus' word, climaxes with the healing of the paralytic. This climax established what Matthew had been showing his readers through this whole section—the authority of Jesus' word proves that He is God.

Mark's introductory summary to the Galilean ministry proclaims the kingdom present. The events that immediately follow serve to illustrate and establish that truth.

Luke begins Jesus' ministry with the visit to Nazareth and the reading of the Isaiah scroll in the synagog. Isaiah's prophecy established Jesus' message and mission as one of release. Using a sequence of events that on the surface looks very much like Mark's, Luke introduced changes that made these events in Jesus' ministry contribute toward his release motif. Thus he developed Jesus' ministry as being one of release for oppressed people.

There are scores of other examples that could be presented, but perhaps what we have set forth is sufficient to show how these men wrote as theologians under the Lucan model of inspiration. We now turn our attention to other things.

Small, Unimportant Changes

Those in the Seventh-day Adventist Church who write apologetically and polemically about inspiration often seem to gloss over differences among the synoptic Gospels. These differences are labeled by them as being "unimportant," or "minor discrepancies," or are classed as being "of a minor order."[1] The reason for labeling these differences in this way is to assure the church that the scriptural message has in no way been affected by these "discrepancies," in other words that the Bible is trustworthy.

I agree with our apologists and polemists that the Bible is indeed trustworthy. But are not the church members done a gross injustice when they are led to believe that the "minor discrepancies" are "unimportant," that they are "of a minor order"? After all, it is through these variations that the gospel writers communicate to us their understanding of Jesus. These "minor discrepancies" just happen to be the touch of the writer's paintbrush to the portrait of Jesus. The purpose of this chapter is to show that no "discrepancy," no matter how "minor," is "unimportant" or "of a minor order."

In a previous chapter we have already noted some of the minor changes made by the synoptic writers. Some of these were merely pointed out; others were examined in greater detail. It is time now to pull a number of these "minor discrepancies" together and to see what role they play in the Lucan model of inspiration.

The gospel record of the healing of Peter's mother-in-law and

71

the miracles performed in Capernaum after sunset provide several of these minor changes. We have already looked at several aspects of this story, but now we shall pursue these minor discrepancies and observe how they contribute to the motif each writer is developing. We shall deal with the healing of Peter's mother-in-law first. Following the pattern we have used before, we shall place the gospel accounts side by side. This will aid us in seeing the small variations.

Matthew	Mark	Luke
And when Jesus entered Peter's house, he saw his mother-in-law lying sick with a fever; he touched her hand, and the fever left her, and she rose and served him (8:14, 15).	And immediately he left the synagogue, and entered the house of Simon and Andrew, with James and John. Now Simon's mother-in-law lay sick with a fever, and immediately they told him of her. And he came and took her by the hand and lifted her up, and the fever left her; and she served them (1:29-31).	And he arose and left the synagogue, and entered Simon's house. Now Simon's mother-in-law was ill with a high fever, and they besought him for her. And he stood over her and rebuked the fever, and it left her; and immediately she rose and served them (4:38, 39).

After examining the three narratives, it would be standard scholarly procedure to say that Matthew gave us the original account of this event, because it is the shortest. Both Mark and Luke added details not found in the gospel of Matthew. Thus, for example, we have already noted that Matthew said nothing about this miracle taking place on the Sabbath, while Mark and Luke told us that this was one of the Sabbath miracles performed by Jesus. As we have already noted, Matthew did not record the healing of the demoniac in the synagogue at Capernaum that preceded Jesus' visit to Peter's home. Therefore, in harmony with his method of presentation Matthew also omitted the fact that this was a Sabbath miracle. He is simply being consistent. Because

Mark and Luke presented the healing of the demoniac in the synagogue, they also informed us that Jesus' visit to Peter's home immediately followed the worship service.

Mark seems to imply that not only Simon was with Jesus, but also Andrew, James, and John. Luke did not do so. What is the significance of this? In Mark Jesus called these four disciples at the beginning of the Galilean ministry. Mark told us that they accompanied Jesus to the synagogue at Capernaum, where Jesus healed the demoniac. They then followed Jesus to Simon's home. So Mark is being consistent also. In Luke, the disciples were not called until after the healing of Peter's mother-in-law. Therefore, Luke could not include them at the synagogue nor could he include Andrew, James, and John at Simon's home. So Luke too is being consistent.

If we may digress a little further: We can see a further example of how these two writers remained consistent within the accounts they presented. Thus, when we come to the experience of the disciples picking grain on the Sabbath, we have the following variation:

Mark	Luke
One sabbath he was going through the grainfields; and as they made their way his disciples began to pluck heads of grain. And the Pharisees said to him, "Look, why are they doing what is not lawful on the sabbath?" (2:23, 24).	On a sabbath, while he was going through the grainfields, his disciples plucked and ate some heads of grain, rubbing them in their hands. But some of the Pharisees said, "Why are you doing what is not lawful to do on the sabbath?" (6:1, 2).

Did you notice that in Mark the Pharisees addressed their question to Jesus, "the Pharisees said to him"? But in Luke the Pharisees addressed the disciples, who were actually plucking the grain, "Why are you doing what is not lawful?" A minor difference, perhaps, but each writer is consistent with the context he presents. How is this so?

Remember, in Mark Jesus called His disciples as He entered upon His Galilean ministry. They accompanied Him into the synagogue at Capernaum on the Sabbath and saw Him exorcise the demon (the first Sabbath miracle recorded by Mark and Luke). Jesus' act of healing would be considered unlawful—a violation of Sabbath restrictions. When the disciples plucked grain on the Sabbath to relieve their hunger, the Pharisees addressed Jesus and demanded an explanation for the disciples' Sabbath violation. By turning upon Jesus, the Pharisees as much as said, "What your disciples are doing is Your fault. You have taught them to ignore Sabbath restrictions!" We see therefore, that on the basis of Jesus' earlier miracle on the Sabbth, the Pharisees were laying the blame for the disciples' misbehavior on the Sabbath at Jesus' door.

In Luke, the disciples had not yet been called by Jesus when He healed the demoniac at Capernaum. Therefore, there was no precedent of a "Sabbath violation" for the disciples to follow. The Pharisees, then, did not lay the blame at Jesus' door. They spoke to the disciples directly and chastized them for yielding to hunger pangs and thus breaking the Sabbath by plucking, winnowing, and grinding the grain.

What have we seen? We have seen several differences that have resulted from the writers' being consistent to alterations they made earlier in their gospel accounts. Therefore, some changes that appear to be "discrepancies" are nothing more than attempts at being consistent.

Let us now return to the healing of Peter's mother-in-law. It is in Luke's account of her healing that we see "minor discrepancies" that play an important role in what Luke is saying. If you will recall our discussion of this miracle in an earlier chapter, Luke added the minor detail that this woman suffered from a "high" fever. Luke also told us that Jesus "rebuked" the fever. That is, He spoke to it as though it possessed intelligence—remember the fever demon? So we see that by these small adjustments in the story, one being simply a single word, Luke used the healing of Peter's mother-in-law to advance his motif of release from the captivity of Satan—minor changes, but very important ones!

Now we are ready to examine the second half of this story. After sunset, a multitude of sick people were brought to Jesus for healing. We need to compare the accounts to find out what happened.

Matthew	Mark	Luke
That evening they brought to him many who were possessed with demons; and he cast out the spirits with a word, and healed all who were sick. This was to fulfil what was spoken by the prophet Isaiah, "He took our infirmities and bore our diseases" (8:16, 17).	That evening, at sundown, they brought to him all who were sick or possessed with demons. And the whole city was gathered together about the door. And he healed many who were sick with various diseases, and cast out many demons; and he would not permit the demons to speak, because they knew him (1:32-34).	Now when the sun was setting, all those who had any that were sick with various diseases brought them to him; and he laid his hands on every one of them and healed them. And demons also came out of many, crying, "You are the Son of God!" But he rebuked them, and would not allow them to speak, because they knew that he was the Christ (4:40, 41).

Matthew alone concluded this story of mass healings with a quote from Isaiah. We have already pointed out the significance of this with respect to the events that he recorded immediately afterward. Because of this, some minor changes are given as points of transition to what comes next. Matthew also made a simple addition that is crucial to the whole motif that he developed in chapter 8. He alone of the gospel writers said that Jesus cast out demons "with a word." A minor variation, to say the least, but it is vital to what Matthew is saying about Jesus. The authority and dynamic power of Jesus' spoken word proved Him to be God.

Luke concluded this night of healing, not with a quote from Isaiah, but by telling us the demons who were exorcised confessed Jesus to be the Son of God. It is interesting that Mark said Jesus would not permit the demons to speak. Luke also said Jesus would not allow them to speak, but not before they identified Jesus as God's Son. This identification reminded Luke's readers that release from Satan's captivity is achieved only by divine intervention. Also, the vanquishing of Satan's kingdom accompanies the establishment of God's kingdom, and this kingdom is established only by the activity of God Himself.

We have spent a good deal of time with the healing of Peter's mother-in-law and the healings that followed after sunset. There are at least two more minor alterations that we noticed in earlier chapters which we shall briefly review to strengthen the point that minor changes should not be brushed aside as insignificant. After so doing we will examine a few examples we have not seen before.

In the story of the cleansing of the leper (Matthew 8:1-4; Mark 1:40-45; Luke 5:12-16), Luke alone told us that the man was full of leprosy. This addition by Luke could be considered as being a minor difference, but it is very important for Luke's motif of release from the power of sin, as we have seen earlier. For this unfortunate victim of leprosy became a type of the human race and its contamination by sin. Within Luke's motif, the addition of the fact that this man was "full of leprosy" is not just a minor, unimportant alteration. It is an important element in Luke's portrait of Jesus.

Matthew's feast presented us with an opportunity to examine another minor discrepancy (Matthew 9:10-13; Mark 2:15-17; Luke 5:29-32). You may recall that Luke added the small detail that the feast was prepared for Jesus, i.e., in His honor. This addition in Luke's gospel consisted of one word, a personal pronoun. But the impact this single word has on the story of Matthew's feast is immense. This feast is now seen as a call of divine love, extended to the most despised stratum of Jewish society. Sitting at a feast that had been spread in honor of Jesus, who had just been shown to be God in the preceding story, these tax collectors and sinners were offered the invitation to enter into the new covenant relationship with Jesus. The simple Greek pronoun *autō* ("for Him") became another key element in Luke's motif of release from sin. A minor variation when compared with Matthew and Mark, who do not have this pronoun, but its presence in Luke has significance.

While speaking of Matthew's feast, we might digress for a moment and take note of a detail that Matthew has, which is not present in Mark and Luke. When Jesus was criticized for eating with tax collectors and sinners, He replied, "Those who are well have no need of a physician, but those who are sick. . . . I came not to call the righteous, but sinners [to repentance]." Matthew 9:12, 13. Matthew divided these two concluding statements by inserting the following between them, "Go learn what this means,'I desire mercy, and not sacrifice.' " Verse 13. When we realize that Matthew's audience were Jews and that Jews were sticklers for rituals and ceremonies, we can better understand how the added statement would speak volumes to them. The Lucan model makes no room for such additions. (See Luke 5:31, 32.) Here we see Matthew's brush at work, adding highlights to his protrait of Jesus.

Examples of minor changes are legion in the synoptic Gospels. A detailed study of them would be exceedingly interesting and would doubtless prove to be very informative for those who are concerned with the problem of inspiration. However, such an analysis must wait for another time. To conclude this chapter, we will look at several minor changes made by Mark and one made by Luke. These changes are important, of course, for what each writer wanted to tell us about Jesus.

We have already examined the healing of the man with the withered hand as reported by Luke. You will recall that this miracle joins two others—the question about fasting and the question of plucking of grain on the Sabbath—and these are used by the synoptic writer to present the motif of release from cultic traditions. We saw that, as a Sabbath miracle, it presented the humanitarian nature of the Sabbath and showed how the Sabbath should be properly kept. Mark introduced an element into this story that is not found in Luke.

The story tells us how Jesus was in a synagogue, and a man with a withered hand was also there. The religious leaders, always critical of His Sabbath keeping, watched Him closely to see whether He would heal on the Sabbath. Knowing this, Jesus told the man to stand forth so everyone could see him. Then Jesus asked the leaders whether it was lawful to do well on the Sabbath or not, to save life or to kill. Now notice what Mark introduces:

Mark	Luke
And he looked around at them with anger, grieved at their hardness of heart, and said to the man, "Stretch out your hand." He stretched it out, and his hand was restored. The Pharisees went out, and immediately held counsel with the Herodians against him, how to destroy him (3:5, 6).	And he looked around on them all, and said to him, "Stretch out your hand." And he did so, and his hand was restored. But they were filled with fury and discussed with one another what they might do to Jesus (6:10, 11).

Mark introduced two elements: First, Jesus reacted to the hardheartedness of the religious leaders with a look of *orgēs*—righteous anger or indignation. This snapshot of Jesus is certainly foreign to the mental picture we usually have of Him. He is generally thought of as the meek and mild One. The One who takes the children into His arms and is moved with compassion when He sees human suffering. Mark alone gives us a glimpse of Jesus that adds a new dimension to our understanding of Him.

Here we see Jesus, the Lord of the Sabbath (Mark 2:28), righteously indignant at the hypocritical abuse of humanity and the sacred hours that were designed by God to be a blessing to humanity. Mark gives us an insight we do not often see in the Gospels.

It is true, when Jesus dealt with wayward men and women who were responsive to Him, He was gentle and loving. But on the other hand, when He had to deal with hardhearted hypocrisy and open resistance to His offer of love, He was firm for what was right and a tower of strength for what was true. Repeatedly the religious leaders found Him to be more than a match for them. He refused to be intimidated; He could not be flattered or coerced into even speaking a word that would support their hypocrisy. Thinking they could bully Him, they found Him the dominant personality. With authority, He expressed His displeasure with their shallow understanding of religion. Mark gave us a glimpse of one of these occasions.

The second element that Mark introduced was the scheming by

the Pharisees and the Herodians to bring about Jesus' death. Matthew supports Mark's report of this conspiracy, but does not mention the Herodians.

Mark gives yet another glimpse of Jesus' firmness in the face of the disciples' reluctance to obey a direct command from Jesus. The occasion was the feeding of the five thousand. According to the Gospel of John, there was a movement by a certain group to take Jesus by force and proclaim Him King. John 6:15. The book *The Desire of Ages*[2] offers some insights that help us to understand what was involved. A popular movement initiated by Judas reached its peak with the feeding of the five thousand. Even the other disciples acted a part in fostering these plans. Those who were pushing the movement saw in Jesus the answer to their national ambitions.

When the fragments of the meal had been collected, those who had instigated the plans to take Jesus decided it was time to make their move. Seeing what was coming, Jesus told the disciples to get into the boat and to set sail for the opposite shore. All the disciples could see was the ruin of their hopes and ambitions. Mark said, "Immediately he made his disciples get into the boat and go before him to the other side, to Bethsaida, while he dismissed the crowd." Mark 6:45.

An inattentive reader can easily miss the significance of what Mark says, for he gives no indication that a plot was unfolding to crown Jesus king by force. But the word *made* should catch our attention. Some years ago I assigned this passage for my intermediate Greek class. The young man who translated this verse during the next class period did a good job. However, when he came to the word *ēnagkasen* ("made, forced, compelled"), he translated it "urged." I asked him why he chose "urged." He told me he had looked the word up in the lexicon, and had chosen *urged* because it was not like Jesus to make or compel anyone to do anything. Then I told him by softening his translation, he missed the whole point that Mark is endeavoring to bring out.

Going back to *The Desire of Ages*, we can see what was unfolding and what was reflected in Mark by his choice of words. A delegation was advancing toward Jesus to take Him by force, if necessary, to make Him King. "Calling His disciples, Jesus bids them take the boat and return at once to Capernaum, leaving Him to dismiss the people.

"Never before had a command from Christ seemed so impossible of fulfillment. . . . They protested against the arrangement; but Jesus now spoke with an authority He had never before assumed toward them. They knew that further opposition on their part would be useless, and in silence they turned toward the sea."[3]

By the use of that one word *make*, Mark projects a picture of One in command. One who possessed a dominant personality and a strong will. One who was not to be manipulated nor resisted. Matthew and Luke did not record the righteous anger of Jesus in the synagogue, nor did Luke record the event by the sea. Matthew, however, joints Mark here and records the fact that Jesus forced the disciples against their will.

Mark once again, at a later point, showed the domanance of Jesus' authority and the power of His will. All three synoptic writers presented the second cleansing of the temple. This act alone showed the authority with which Jesus acted against those who profaned the worship of God. But Mark added what might be thought by some as a minor point, which in reality is significant.

Once Jesus had cleansed the temple, Mark said, "He would not allow any one to carry anything through the temple." Mark 11:16. Here we see One in total control of what took place in the temple. Jesus dictated what was permissible and what was not. When you understand what had gone on in the temple courts before the cleansing, you can see how dominant Jesus' will was. He brought all of the corrupt proceedings to an abrupt end, and in the face of the most powerful religious and social forces of His day, He did not allow these proceedings to resume, so long as He was there. For the time being, Jesus took complete control of the temple and dominated its services.

The KJV renders a truer translation of this interesting verse in Mark, "And [He] would not suffer that any man should carry any vessel through the temple." Werner Kelber sees *vessel* as referring to the temple services. He asks, "What other significance can *skeuos*, vessel, in conjunction with *to hieron*, temple, have but that of a sacred cult vessel?"[4] Therefore, Kelber concludes that

Jesus shut the whole temple down, not only the illicit traffic in the outer court, but also the sacrifices and the services. This, to me, seems extreme. However, there is no question but what Jesus was in control of the temple and had snatched away from the priests authority over its proceeding. Only Mark gives us these details in his portrait of Jesus.

We will notice one more "minor discrepancy" found in Luke. When Jesus died, a Roman officer, who had been in command of the execution, spoke his feelings about all that he had witnessed. The testimony of this pagan soldier stands in bold contrast to the attitude of the religious leaders. But notice the discrepancy:

Matthew	Mark	Luke
When the centurion and those who were with him, keeping watch over Jesus, saw the earthquake and what took place, they were filled with awe, and said, "Truly this was the Son of God!" (27:54).	And when the centurion, who stood facing him, saw that he thus breathed his last, he said, "Truly this man was the Son of God!" (15:39).	Now when the centurion saw what had taken place, he praised God, and said, "Certainly this man was innocent!" (23:47).

"Son of God" or "innocent"? Luke changed what Matthew and Mark reported by the use of a single word. Surely a minor discrepancy, but as we shall see, a very important one. The statement of the centurion fits into a series of alterations made by Luke that present to us his understanding of the rejection of Jesus by the religious leaders. The importance of what the centurion said is seen by way of contrast. The religious leaders saw Jesus as guilty and deserving death. The Roman centurion represented the position of the pagan Roman government—Jesus was innocent of any crime worthy of death. A minor change as far as the wording is concerned, but a major change in thought content.

Now, what have we seen in this chapter? We have become very much aware of small changes made by the synoptic writers. Some changes involve a sentence or a clause, others a mere word. But each change makes a contribution to what the writer is saying about Jesus. It is my hope that the next time the Gospels are read, these "minor discrepancies" will be noted and the messages they convey will be appreciated. After all, they are the touch of the writer's paintbrush.

References

1. Warren H. Johns, "Scripture Is by Inspiration of God," *Ministry,* 54 (March 1981), p. 18; William G. Johnsson, "How Does God Speak?" *Ministry,* 54 (October 1981), p. 6.

2. Ellen G. White, *The Desire of Ages* (Mountain View, Calif.: Pacific Press Publishing Association, 1940), pp. 718, 377, 378.

3. *Ibid.,* p. 378.

4. Werner Kelber, *The Kingdom in Mark* (Philadelphia: Fortress Press, 1974), p. 101.

Large, Important Changes

The "minor discrepancies" we have been investigating in the last chapter are, as a rule, not dealt with in detail by commentators, although some may mention them. Thus, for example, it is true that Luke's statement that the leper was "full" of leprosy attracts the attention of some scholars. Some of these may even compare Luke's statement with those of Matthew and Mark and note the difference, but seldom if ever is any attempt made to see how this addition aids in the development of Luke's theme. On the other hand, little, if anything, is made of the fact that Matthew's feast was given in honor of Jesus, or as he puts it, "for him." We recognize, of course, the various objectives of commentators will dictate what they emphasize in their commentaries. Although this book is not a commentary, there are a number of minor variations in the material that we have examined thus far concerning which nothing has been said. Possibly another writer would have chosen to deal with these other "minor discrepancies" and to ignore the ones that are presented here.

However, when it comes to major changes that are obvious to the majority of readers, most every Bible commentator pauses to say a word or two about them. In this chapter, we shall examine two such alterations—the call to discipleship and the anointing of Jesus' feet. They both present the same significant challenges: (1) Luke moves them out of the time frames in which we find them in Matthew and Mark, and (2) they have obviously been completely rewritten. Here again, we will see that only the Lucan model of inspiration can adequately account for such an occurrence.

We have already examined the call of the first disciples and noted that it has been relocated by Luke in an entirely different setting, and that Peter's confession of his sinfulness is the major point of the story. What we did not then stress, and what we need to stress now, is how extensive the relocations and the rewritings are.

First, we will review the extent of its relocation. Again, the easiest way to see what has happened is to line up the stories as they appear in the synoptics.

Matthew	Mark	Luke
Introductory statement to Galilean ministry (4:12-17)	Introductory statement to Galilean ministry (1:14, 15)	Introductory statement to Galilean ministry (4:14, 15)
Call of first disciples (4:18-22)	Call of first disciples (1:16-20)	
Summary statement on ministry (4:23-25)		
Sermon on the Mount (5-7)		Visit to Nazareth (4:16-30)
	Demoniac at Capernaum (1:21-18)	Demoniac at Capernaum (4:31-37)
	Healing many people (1:29-34)	Healing many people (4:38-41)
	A preaching tour (1:35-39)	A preaching tour (4:42-44)
		Call of first disciples (5:1-11)

There is no question but that the relocation of the call to discipleship is a major piece of surgery performed by Luke. All we have to do is to glance at the three columns and any observer is almost forced to exclaim, What has happened? Obviously the prophetic model of inspiration is inadequate to answer such a pointed question.

Understanding what Luke has done would be difficult enough if he had taken the call of the first disciples as it reads in Matthew and Mark and had moved it to its present location in his Gospel. But Luke compounds the difficulty by rewriting the story. This becomes obvious when we compare the three accounts. To give the accounts here word by word would be too unwieldy, I shall therefore simply list the main points of each story as it appears in the synoptics.

Matthew	Mark	Luke
Jesus walked by the sea	Jesus walked by the sea	People pressed upon Jesus as He taught by the lake
Peter and Andrew were casting a net	Simon and Andrew were casting a net	Jesus got into Simon's boat and taught from there
Jesus said, "Follow Me"	Jesus said, "Follow Me"	When finished Jesus told Simon to put out into the deep to fish
They followed	They followed	
A little farther Jesus saw James and John	A little farther Jesus saw James and John	Simon objected
They were mending nets	They were mending nets	When he obeyed, he caught a large school of fish
Jesus called them	Jesus called them	Simon called for help
They followed (4:18-22)	They followed (1:16-20)	Filled two boats
		Simon confessed his sinfulness
		Jesus called Simon and partners to discipleship (5:1-11)

A careful reading of the gospel accounts shows no obvious similarity between the call of the disciples as recorded by Matthew and Mark, on the one hand, and the one by Luke on the other. The two problems, the relocation of the event and the rewriting of what happened, have caused a great deal of discussion among New Testament scholars. Some of these scholars have said that there must have been two distinct calls given by Jesus to the very same men. Their theory is as follows: Matthew and Mark reported the first of these calls. This call led to a part-time relationship with Jesus. In other words, the disciples continued to periodically return to their occupation of fishing. Luke, on the other hand, recorded the second call. This call resulted in a full-time relationship with Jesus.[1]

But not all scholars agree with this latter theory. Thus, for example, F. Godet states that he is hard pressed to see two separate calls made to the very same men. Especially so since Jesus said He would make them fishers of men, and in turn they responded twice by leaving all in order to follow Him. Therefore, Godet concludes that what we have here is two differing accounts of the same call.[2]

Another scholar thinks Luke combined two different stories. He took the miracle story about the large catch of fish and put Mark's call to discipleship at the conclusion.[3] Still others think that Luke borrowed the story from John 21, where Jesus, after His resurrection, prepared breakfast for the disciples while they were out fishing once again.[4] On the other hand, some think the differences between the story in John and the story in Luke are too great for one to be borrowed from the other.[5] And so the discussion goes on.

However, it is the opinion of this author that Luke's use of the call to discipleship is carefully planned. Its relocation after certain other events allowed Luke to introduce the problem of sin, an element that is not present in Mark's sequence. The differing account, with Peter's confession of his sinfulness, allows Luke to continue to develop the motif of release by introducing release from the power of sin. This motif is missing in Mark's sequence. There are two reasons for this: (1) Mark does not have Jesus' visit to Nazareth at this point, nor the reading of the Isaiah scroll which proclaims the Messiah's mission of release.

We might just note here that Mark does record a visit to Nazareth by Jesus at a later point in his Gospel. See Mark 6:1-6. However, there is a strong possibility that this is a second visit and not the one reported by Luke. (2) The second reason that the motif of release is missing in Mark at this point in his sequence is that he used these same stories to establish the truth of Jesus' proclamation as He entered Galilee, "The time is fulfilled, and the kingdom of God is at hand [is present]." Mark 1:15.

If we were to place the call of discipleship under the umbrella of the prophetic model, we would have to ask, Which of the gospel accounts is true? In other words, if God showed Matthew and Mark that Jesus called the first disciples at the beginning of the Galilean ministry, how could He possibly show Luke that Jesus called the very same disciples at a later time? If God showed to Matthew and Mark in vision that Jesus called the disciples from casting and mending nets, how could He possibly show Luke that Jesus and Simon went on a fishing trip? In other words, if what Matthew and Mark recorded is the truth about the call of the first disciples, then what Luke recorded is not, and vice versa. This is a problem that has perplexed many earnest Bible students. The prophetic model cannot account for what has happened to the story of the call to discipleship.

The Lucan model of inspiration that we are proposing allows us to work out a satisfactory solution to this puzzling problem. Perhaps referring again to a scenario will help. Mark, as a *hupēretēs,* had memorized the call to discipleship just as we find it it recorded by Matthew and himself. Peter and Andrew were casting a net and James and John were mending their nets when Jesus appeared by the seaside. But Mark did not tell the entire story. He had memorized an abbreviated account only. However Luke in writing his gospel uncovered further details in his research, either from an eyewitness, another *hupēretēs,* or from another gospel, and he included these in his account.

Luke filled in a number of details omitted by Matthew and Mark. The call may have happened like this. As Jesus made His way along the shore of the Sea of Galilee teaching the people, the crowd began to increase in numbers. No one wanted to miss a word of Jesus' discourse and they began to "press upon" Him to catch all that He said. Coming upon Simon and Andrew casting their net, Jesus stepped into their boat and asked Simon to push out from the shore a few feet. From this vantage point, Jesus continued teaching. When He concluded His instruction, He told Simon and Andrew to move out into the lake and to let down their net. It is at this point that we have the miracle of the large catch of fish followed by Simon's confession. In the meantime, James and John had been mending their nets with their father. If they stopped their work to listen to Jesus teach, Luke does not inform us. But when Peter called for help, they responded at once.

The Lucan model of inspiration can reasonably account for the difference in the two versions of the same incident when we realize there are no visions involved. Instead what we have is the collection (as a result of research) and use of information. The Lucan model of inspiration will also allow the relocation of this story; for, as a theologian, Luke used it to expand his understanding of the mission of Jesus as it is proclaimed in the Isaiah scroll, i.e., release.

What has happened to the story of the call of the disciples also happened to the story of the woman who anointed Jesus' feet. It has been moved by Luke from the last week of Jesus' life and has been placed back into His Galilean ministry. This involves a move that covers more than a year—a surgery that is even more radical than the relocation of the call to discipleship. Besides this, the account found in Luke is as completely rewritten as is the call to discipleship.

As we look at the relocation the story of the woman who anointed Jesus' feet, we must call upon the Gospel of John for help. By reading the accounts of Matthew, Mark, and John, it is clear that they place this anointing of Jesus during the last week of His earthly life. However, when we compare these three gospel accounts, we come up with a second chronological problem. This will have to be solved before we can return to Luke. So let us compare these gospels and identify the problem.

Matthew	Mark	John
When Jesus had finished all these sayings, he said to his disciples, "You know that after two days the Passover is coming, and the Son of man will be delivered up to be crucified." Then the chief priests and the elders of the people gathered in the palace of the high priest, who was called Caiaphas, and took counsel together in order to arrest Jesus by stealth and kill him. But they said, "Not during the feast, lest there be a tumult among the people." Now when Jesus was at Bethany in the house of Simon the leper, a woman came up to him with an alabaster flask of very expensive ointment (26:1-7).	It was now two days before the Passover and the feast of Unleavened Bread. And the chief priests and the scribes were seeking how to arrest him by stealth, and kill him; for they said, "Not during the feast, lest there be a tumult of the people." And while he was at Bethany in the house of Simon the leper, as he sat at table, a woman came with an alabaster flask of pure nard (14:1-3).	Six days before the Passover, Jesus came to Bethany, where Lazarus was, whom Jesus had raised from the dead. There they made him a supper; Martha served, and Lazarus was one of those at table with him. Mary took a pound of costly ointment of pure nard (12:1-3).

As we read these three accounts, the problem immediately becomes apparent. Did this anointing of Jesus take place six days before the Passover or was it two? If you read the accounts of Matthew and Mark carefully, it soon becomes apparent that the time period of two days does not refer to the anointing. This is the reason we have to call on John's witness. In his gospel Mark said, "It was now two days before the Passover. . . . And the chief priests and scribes were seeking how to arrest him." Mark 14:1. Clearly the two days in Mark are attached to the attempt of the religious leaders to arrest Jesus, not to the anointing. This point becomes apparent by the way Mark begins his version of the anointing episode with the words, "And while he was at Bethany." Verse 3.

Matthew's account is a little more difficult to explain than that of Mark. The two days before the Passover appear to be attached to the apocalyptic discourse Jesus delivered to His disciples on the Mount of Olives, which we find recorded in chapters 24 and 25. After the parable of the sheep and the goats, which concluded this apocalyptic discourse, Matthew said, "When Jesus had finished all these sayings, he said to his disciples, 'You know that after two days the Passover is coming.' " Matthew 26:1, 2. These two days do not seem to refer to the meeting of the religious leaders, as they do in Mark, nor do they refer to the anointing by the woman. So we see that neither in Matthew nor in Mark does the time period of two days before the Passover refer to the anointing of Jesus. It seems evident, therefore, that we must depend on John's chronology which seems to be more exact and conclude that it must have taken place six days before the Passover. In other words, the annointing took place within the last week of Jesus' life.

We have examined enough of the Lucan model of inspiration to realize that Luke is trying to communicate something to us by moving the story of Jesus' anointing from the time period specified by Matthew, Mark, and John back into the Galilean ministry. This, in turn, becomes all the more obvious as we examine the story in its rewritten form. What is it he is saying about Jesus? We can find out by comparing Luke with Matthew and Mark. Again it would be too unwieldy if all three accounts were given word for word, so again we summarize.

Matthew	Mark	Luke
Jesus in Bethany at home of Simon the leper	Jesus in Bethany at home of Simon the leper	Jesus invited to meal by a Pharisee
A woman anointed His head as He sat at table	A woman anointed His head as He sat at table	A sinful woman entered and anointed His feet, weeping on them and wiping them with her hair and kissing them
Disciples indignant, "Why this waste?"	Disciples indignant, "Why this waste?" They reproached her	Pharisee said, "If this man were a prophet He would know this woman is a sinner."
Jesus said, "Why trouble the woman? She has done a beautiful thing to me. She has anointed my body for the burial. What she has done will be told as a memory of her" (26:6-13).	Jesus said, "Let her alone. She has done a beautiful thing to me. She has anointed my body for burying. What she has done will be told in memory of her" (14:3-9).	Jesus told Simon a parable of two debtors. One owed much, the other little
		They were both forgiven
		Jesus asked, "Which one will love the most?"
		Simon replied, "The one forgiven the most."
		Jesus said, "You are right. I entered your home and you extended to me no courtesy. This woman has shown courtesy."
		Jesus said to the woman, "Your sins are forgiven; your faith has saved you. Go in peace" (7:36-50).

Here we see an entirely different account in which the disciples play no role and the host, Simon, plays a major part. As with the call to discipleship, there is a great deal of debate as to whether we have one event or two. Especially when the woman anoints Jesus' head in Matthew and Mark and His feet in Luke. Because Luke does not report this story in the place where Matthew and Mark recorded it, John Creed believes it is a variation of Mark 14:3-9. Creed says that Luke probably drew upon another source, other than Mark, to gain this information.[6] Therefore, Creed sees Matthew, Mark, and Luke as reporting the same event. Others disagree and say we have two entirely different events.[7] Obviously I agree with Creed. Luke used a report of an eyewitness or of another *hupēretēs* to fill in the details missing in Matthew and Mark. On the other hand, the details reported by Matthew and Mark were omitted by Luke because he used this story for a different purpose than the other two synoptic writers.

This brings us to the important question, Why did Luke rewrite and relocate the story of Jesus' anointing? Commentators have quickly pointed out the obvious, "The real intention of vv 44-47 is to point the broad contrast between the response of the sinner and the response of the Pharisee to the divine teacher."[8]

The woman and the Pharisee become symbols. The woman represents the common people and those who were despised by the religious leaders. She also is a representative of how these two classes of people responded to Jesus and His teaching. The Pharisee represents the response of the religious leadership. The woman had found in Jesus' words the way of life, and in Jesus a personal Saviour. Her expression of love and gratitude was shown in the pouring forth of the expensive ointment. The Pharisee withheld from Jesus common courtesies. "You gave me no water for my feet," Jesus said. Verse 44. "You gave me no kiss." Verse 45. "You did not anoint my head with oil." Verse 46.

William F. Arndt says, "The Pharisee had treated Jesus as an inferior."[9] By rewriting this story, Luke is expressing more than that; he is contrasting the two attitudes of acceptance by the common people and rejection on the part of the religious leaders, of whom Simon was the representative.

How, then, does the relocation of this story help Luke to show this attitude of rejection? He has moved it into a position where it concluded a series of three events that center on the theme of rejection: (1) the healing of the centurion's servant (7:1-10), (2) the raising of the widow's son at Nain (7:11-17) as it complements Jesus' response to (3) the messengers from John the Baptist (7:18-35).

The way Jesus dealt with the repentant woman in this story presents two secondary motifs. First, Jesus showed respect for women. He did not treat them as being of less importance than men, which was the general attitude of the male population in Jesus' society. In fact, Jesus' dealings with women were of interest to Luke, for he repeatedly recorded how Jesus related to all classes of people who were despised by the religious leaders. It is Luke who tells us that Jesus allowed certain women to travel with His group. This gave them an opportunity to perform a ministry that aided Jesus and His disciples in their work. Luke 8:1-3.

Second, this story showed Jesus' compassion for sinners. The woman that anointed Jesus was labeled as "a sinner" by society. Simon's attitude toward her indicated that because of her sins she was an outcast from Jewish society. Jesus, on the other hand, had forgiven her sins. The attention of the assembled guests was directed to her when He said to Simon, "Do you see this woman?" Luke 7:44. He then proceeded to point out the evidence of her great love. When Jesus said to the woman, "Your sins are forgiven. . . . Your faith has saved you; go in peace" (verses 48-50), the Saviour publicly lifted this woman to respectability and restored her to society. No longer could anyone refer to her in contempt as "a sinner."

Thus we can say this one story contains three motifs. The contrast between the response of the woman to Jesus and the response of Simon is the major motif. It was the development of this motif of rejection that led Luke to relocate this event and rewrite it. However, the rewriting of this story presents two minor motifs, (1) Jesus' relation to and dealing with women, and (2) His great compassion for sinners.

The foregoing stresses an important fact of the Lucan model of inspiration. More than one theme can often be found in any one story. Each theme is developed as the gospel story progresses. At one point a theme may receive major emphasis, as the rejection of Jesus does at Simon's feast. At another point the very same theme may receive minor treatment. But these minor touches make a contribution to the overall theme as it proceeds through the gospel story. Once one is aware of the Lucan model, he watches for the development of themes as they appear in major and minor roles in various stories.

It is interesting to discover the use made of the anointing of Jesus in Matthew and Mark, as well as noticing what Luke has inserted into the place from which the anointing was removed. In fact, the replacement in Luke helps us understand the purpose for which the anointing is used to Matthew and Mark.

When we compare these two Gospels, we find that the sequence of events are the same, but some of the details differ. We do not have time now to pursue all of the "minor discrepancies," but you are aware now that these serve a purpose for the writer. At this point we can only stress the use made of the anointing. Following Jesus' apocalyptic sermon on the end of the world, both writers tell us of a meeting convened by the religious leaders. The purpose of this meeting was to plot their strategy to put Jesus to death. It is clear from the two accounts the leaders were in a dilemma. If they were to take Jesus by stealth, they needed inside help. The report of this meeting is followed by the anointing of Jesus and then by Judas' offer to the chief priests to betray His Lord. It is clear that these three events go together as a unit. Matthew 26:1-16; Mark 14:1-11.

How, then, does the anointing of Jesus fit into the intrigue? When Jesus was anointed by the woman, it was the disciples who found fault with what she had done. Remember, in Luke's account it was Simon. However, in all three accounts Jesus spoke to those who criticized her actions. In Luke, Jesus spoke to Simon. In Matthew and Mark, He spoke to the disciples.

Jesus' response to the disciples' criticism in Matthew was one of firm correction, "Why do you trouble the woman? For she has done a beautiful thing to me. For you always have the poor with you, but you will not always have me." Matthew 26:10, 11. In Mark, the scene is intensified. After the disciples indignantly asked why the ointment was wasted on Jesus, Mark added, "They reproached her." Mark 14:5. Jesus' response was sharpened to meet this intensified criticism, "Let her alone; why do you trouble her?" Verse 6. Following this confrontation between Jesus and His disciples, Judas went to the chief priests and offered his services as a betrayer. Matthew 26:14-16; Mark 14:10, 11.

It becomes clear by examining the two accounts that Jesus' rebuke of the disciples motivated Judas to betray his Lord. He provided what the religious leaders needed if Jesus was to be taken by stealth, through an "inside-contact man." Therefore, the anointing of Jesus in Matthew and Mark served to provide the betrayer that the religious leaders needed to accomplish their deadly purpose. This is an entirely different function for this event than the function it has in Luke.

Luke, of course, having talked to Mark, the *hupēretēs,* was aware that as a result of Jesus' sharp rebuke, Judas was offended, after which he decided to seek revenge by betraying Jesus. But once he had moved the story of the anointing of Jesus to another location to serve another purpose, how was the betrayer to be provided?

When we look at Luke's account, we see that when he came to the place in the story where the anointing stood in Matthew and Mark, he provided a second reason for Judas' betrayal: "Now the feast of Unleaven Bread drew near, which is called the Passover. And the chief priests and the scribes were seeking how to put him to death; for they feared the people. Then Satan entered into Judas called Iscariot, who was of the number of the twelve; he went away and conferred with the chief priests and officers how he might betray him to them." Luke 22:1-4.

Realizing that a reason had to be given for one of Jesus' disciples turning against Him, and having already used the cause for the betrayal for another purpose, Luke simply said, "Satan entered into Judas." The Gospel of John helps us here, for John tells us specifically that it was Judas who was the originator of the criticism that was directed toward the woman and that Jesus' rebuke was directed toward Judas. John 12:4-8.

What have we seen in this chapter? As the small, unnoticed changes play an important role in the Lucan model of inspiration, so the large, obvious changes have a role to play. They are all highlights that enable us to see Jesus through the writer's eyes.

References

1. William F. Arndt, *The Gospel According to St. Luke* (St. Louis: Concordia Publishing House, 1956), pp. 155, 156; and Norval Geldenhuys, *Commentary on the Gospel of Luke* (Grand Rapids, Mich.: William B. Eerdmans Publishing Company, 1954), pp. 1980-1981.

2. F. Godet, *A Commentary on the Gospel of St. Luke*, trans. by E. W. Shalders, 5th ed. (Edinburgh: T & T Clark, [1952]), 1:255.

3. I. Howard Marshall, *The Gospel of Luke: A Commentary on the Greek Text* (Grand Rapids, Mich.: William B. Eerdmans Publishing Company, 1978), pp. 199-201; cf. I. Howard Marshall, *Luke: Historian and Theologian* (Grand Rapids, Mich.: Zondervan Publishing House, 1971), p. 65.

4. John Martin Creed, *The Gospel According to St. Luke* (London: Macmillan and Company, Ltd., 1960), pp. 73, 74; Burton Scott Easton, *The Gospel According to St. Luke: A Critical and Exegetical Commentary* (Edinburgh: T & T Clark, 1926), p. 62; J. Alexander Findlay, *The Gospel According to St. Luke* (London: Student Christian Movement Press, 1937), p. 69; C. G. Montefiore, *The Synoptic Gospels* (London: Macmillan and Company, Ltd., 1909), 2:879.

5. G. B. Caird, *The Gospel of St. Luke* (Baltimore: Penguin Books, 1963), p. 91; Alfred Plummer, *A Critical and Exegetical Commentary of the Gospel According to St. Luke* (Edinburgh: T & T Clark, 1913), p. 147.

6. Creed, p. 109.

7. Arndt, p. 218; Plummer, p. 214; and Summers, p. 89.

8. Creed, p. 109; cf. Plummer, p. 210.

9. Arndt, p. 220.

Luke's View of Salvation

Throughout the preceding chapters we have spoken of motifs that have been developed within passages, or groups of passages, that stand side by side. One of the longest motifs that we have examined has been that of release, which was introduced by the reading of the Isaiah scroll in the synagogue at Nazareth. We saw how Luke used the material that immediately followed the visit to Nazareth to develop the motifs of release from the captivity of Satan, release from the power of sin, and release from cultic traditions. These three motifs, in turn, explain how Luke understood the overall theme of release as presented by the Isaiah scroll.

In this chapter, we shall examine a single motif and see how it runs through a gospel book. There are a number of such motifs that we can choose from. In another work, I have shown how the motif of rejection runs through the book of Luke.[1] Although it was not my intention to develop this motif at that time to its fullest extent, a reader can see how a gospel writer pursued a motif, presenting it as the dominant theme in one passage and as a secondary theme in another passage.

The motif of salvation is a major theme that is present in all three synoptics. But each synoptic writer develops it in his own way. There are a number of statements made by Jesus concerning salvation that are common to all three writers. Then there are statements and events recorded by one writer that cannot be found in the others. It is these additions by the single writer that we will examine and that will help us to see how he develops a motif so that it becomes uniquely his own.

7—L.A.P.

We are going to concentrate on the Gospel of Luke to see how the Lucan model of inspiration will allow him, as an author and a theologian, to develop his own understanding of Jesus as Saviour. We will begin with the birth of Jesus. As we go along, notice how often the main characters in Luke's birth story speak of salvation.

The motif of salvation is introduced early by Luke, and it becomes the dominant theme in his birth account. For example, when the angel Gabriel appeared to Zachariah to announce the birth of John, he told Zachariah that John would function in the role of Elijah. In this role, John would lead "many" in Israel into a new experience of salvation, "And he will turn many of the sons of Israel to the Lord their God, . . . to make ready for the Lord a people prepared." Luke 1:16, 17.

Then when Mary visited Elizabeth, she praised God in the beautiful hymn that has been called the Magnificat, "My soul magnifies the Lord, and my spirit rejoices in God my Savior." Luke 1:46, 47. She then speaks of God's mercy being extended to her as a humble handmaid, and proceeds to tell how God's mercy will be shown to Israel through the fulfillment of the covenant promises made with Abraham. Verses 48-55. The whole hymn speaks of God's work of salvation.

When the time had arrived for the naming of John, the tongue of Zachariah, his father, was loosed, and, filled with the Holy Spirit, he prophesied, "Blessed be the God of Israel, for he has visited and redeemed his people, and has raised up a horn of salvation for us in the house of his servant David." Luke 1:68, 69. This salvation is set within the context of the mercies promised to the fathers in the covenant God swore to Abraham. Verses 72, 73. John would prepare the way before the Lord, "to give knowledge of salvation to his people in the forgiveness of their sins, . . . to give light to those who sit in darkness and in the shadow of death." Verses 77-79.

With the words of the angel to Zachariah and the hymns of Mary and Zachariah, the stage is now set for the entrance of the main character in the drama of salvation: "I bring you good news of a great joy which will come to all the people; for to you is born this day in the city of David a Savior, who is Christ the Lord." Luke 2:10, 11.

When Joseph and Mary took the infant Jesus to the temple for the dedication services, the aged Simeon took the child in his arms and said, "Lord, now lettest thou thy servant depart in peace, according to thy word; for mine eyes have seen thy salvation which thou has prepared in the presence of all peoples." Verses 29-31. Anna the prophetess, having seen the child, spoke about Him "to all who were looking for the redemption of Jerusalem." Verse 38.

All of the above is unique to Luke; Matthew and Mark report none of it. There is no question that as a theologian Luke was interested in the saving act of God. As a writer this interest is brought out in the stories of Zachariah, Mary, the shepeherds, Simeon, and Anna.

When we compare the birth narrative in Luke with that of Matthew we see an interesting reversal. Luke's major interest is salvation, as we have just seen. However, he also introduces a secondary motif that will be expanded later in his Gospel. This secondary motif is the kingship of Jesus. When Gabriel appeared to Mary to talk with her concerning God's proposed plan for bringing the Saviour into the world, Gabriel spoke in terms of kingship, "The Lord God will give to him the throne of his father David, and he will reign over the house of Jacob for ever; and of his kingdom there will be no end." Luke 1:32, 33.

Kingship is introduced briefly into the hymn of Zachariah, "The Lord God . . . has raised up a horn of salvation for us in the house of his servant David." Luke 1:69. It is also alluded to in the words of the angel to the shepherds, "to you is born this day in the city of David a Savior." Luke 2:11. On the basis of Jesus' cleansing and occupying of the temple during the last week of His life, which was the first act Jesus performed as King,[2] there may be implications concerning kingship in Luke's account of Jesus' first visit to the temple as a child. Especially if we accept the RSV's translation of Jesus' words, "How is it that you sought me? Did you not know that I must be in my Father's house?" Luke 2:49.

In Matthew's birth story we find the reverse. Jesus' kingship is the primary motif, and Jesus as Saviour is secondary. For example, Matthew begins his Gospel with a statement of kingship, "The book of the genealogy of Jesus Christ [Messiah, i.e., King], the Son of David." Matthew 1:1. As we have pointed out earlier, this statement is followed by the genealogy with the line of the kings of Judah. Verses 2-16. When the wise men arrive in Jerusalem, they ask, "Where is he who has been born king of the Jews?" Matthew 2:2. Subsequently Herod attempted to eliminate the newborn King. Matthew 2:3-18.

Only in a secondary way does Matthew deal with Jesus as the Saviour in the birth story. The angel Gabriel said to Joseph, "You shall call his name Jesus, for he will save his people from their sins." Matthew 1:21. This is the only reference in Matthew's birth story to Jesus' role as Saviour. Here again we see these men working as individual authors and theologians.

Once we move from the birth story to the ministry of John the Baptist, we see Luke developing the motif of salvation in a way in which it is not done by Matthew and Mark. Luke's interest becomes apparent when we compare the Old Testament quotation that is used to introduce John's ministry.

Matthew	Mark	Luke
The voice of one crying in the wilderness: Prepare the way of the Lord, make his paths straight (3:3).	Behold, I send my messenger before thy face, who shall prepare thy way; the voice of one crying in the wilderness: Prepare the way of the Lord, make his paths straight (1:2, 3).	The voice of one crying in the wilderness: Prepare the way of the Lord, make his paths straight. Every valley shall be filled, and every mountain and hill shall be brought low, and the crooked shall be made straight, and the rough ways shall be made smooth; and all flesh shall see the salvation of God (3:4-6).

All three writers quote from Isaiah 40:3-5, Luke more extensively than Matthew and Mark. However, the closing words of the quotation in Luke are adjusted to fit into his interest. This can be seen when we compare the original words of Isaiah with the way Luke quotes him.

Isaiah	Luke
And the glory of the Lord shall be revealed, and all flesh shall see it together (40:5).	And all flesh shall see the salvation of God (3:6).

That Luke wished to emphasize salvation is very clear. On the other hand, Matthew and Mark did not wish to stress the motif of salvation with these words from Isaiah. They stressed John's role as the forerunner only. Luke used the ministry of John to develop the motif of salvation in another way. His second approach is tied into the motif of rejection, a motif which Luke also develops in his own unique fashion. We will take note of it here only, simply because it ties in momentarily to the motif of salvation. We must again compare what Luke and Matthew say.

Matthew	Luke
But when he saw many of the Pharisees and Sadducees coming for baptism, he said to them, "You brood of vipers! Who warned you to flee from the wrath to come?" (3:7).	He said therefore to the multitudes that came out to be baptized by him, "You brood of vipers! Who warned you to flee from the wrath to come?" (3:7).

The difference is obvious. In Matthew, John called the Pharisees and Sadducees who came to him for baptism a "brood of vipers." In Luke, the religious leaders did not come to John for baptism, so he addresses the crowds as vipers. Of course, someone may say, "The religious leaders could have been among the crowds that John called vipers in Luke's account." This is absolutely true. They could have been in the crowd that flocked to the Jordan, but the point we need to see is that Luke, as an author, does not recognize their presence. If we had Luke's account alone, we would not have known that they came out to John. What does this tell us that Matthew's account does not tell us? It tells us that the religious leaders rejected John as the forerunner of the Messiah. They also rejected his baptism and his message.

This is emphasized by Luke in a later chapter. After the messengers of John the Baptist left Jesus to report to John in prison what they had seen and heard concerning Jesus' ministry (7:18-23), Jesus began to praise John as a prophet: "What did you go out into the wilderness to behold? A reed shaken by the wind? What then did you go out to see? A man clothed in soft clothing? Behold, those who are gorgeously appareled and live in luxury are in kings' courts. What then did you go out to see? A prophet? Yes, I tell you, and more than a prophet. This is he of whom it is written, 'Behold, I send my messenger before thy face, who shall prepare thy way before thee.' " Verses 24-27. Luke alone interjected the following words into Jesus' statement about John: "When they heard this all the people and the tax collectors justified God, having been baptized with the baptism of John; but the Pharisees and the lawyers rejected the purpose of God for themselves, not having been baptized by him." Verses 29, 30. This statement is consistent with Luke's account of John's ministry—no religious leaders are reported as coming to John for baptism.

However, Matthew's statement that the religious leaders came to John for baptism is qualified at a later point by Matthew himself. In 21:23-32, he states twice that the religious leaders did not believe John's message nor did they accept his ministry.

What does the religious leaders' rejection of John and his baptism have to do with the motif of salvation? If we return to John's ministry as reported by Luke, we can see the link between the motif of rejection and the motif of salvation. The link between the two is seen by way of contrast. After the viper statement, Luke says that the multitudes, the publicans, and the soldiers came to John asking, "What shall we do?" Luke 3:10, 12, 14. That this question is to be understood as relating to salvation is apparent in some manuscripts of the Western text which add an additional phrase to the question, so that it reads, "What shall we do so that we might be saved?"

What is clear here is that Luke reports three groups in society who were seeking the way of salvation—the crowds, publicans, and soldiers—while the religious leaders were absent. They did not even come to hear John's message, let alone ask, "What shall we do?"

When we move into chapter 4 of Luke, we find Jesus in the synagogue at Nazareth. Here He read the Isaiah scroll which introduces the motif of release. We have already seen in detail how Luke developed this motif in the events that immediately follow. What we need to point out here is that the motif of release (release from the captivity of Satan, release from the power of sin, and release from cultic tradition) is a part of and a complement to the larger and broader motif of salvation. Release from the captivity of Satan is salvation. Likewise, release from the power of sin and release from cultic traditions are salvation experiences.

In the preceding chapter we saw how Luke relocated and rewrote the incident of the anointing of Jesus. Luke 7:36-50. The relocation and rewriting of this event aids Luke in the development of the rejection motif. The attitude of Simon the Pharisee (only Luke tells us that he was a Pharisee) represents the attitude of the religious leadership. Simon failed to provide the courtesies that one would expect for a guest of honor. William F. Arndt says, "The Pharisee had treated Jesus as an inferior."[3] The woman, on the other hand, provided what the Pharisee refused to give. She represented the various classes that accepted Jesus and heard Him gladly. The attitude of rejection on the part of the Pharisee becomes apparent when contrasted with that of the woman.

Luke's rewritten account of the anointing is placed at the conclusion of a series of other events that show rejection by way of contrast. For example, the conclusion to the sermon on the plain presents two groups: One hears Jesus' words and obeys them; the other hears His words and does not obey them. Luke 6:46-49.

The next event that Luke recorded is the healing of the centurion's servant. When Jesus beheld the faith of the centurion, He said to the crowd that followed Him, "I tell you, not even in Israel have I found such faith." Luke 7:9. This is followed by the rejection of the ministries of John and Jesus. Verses 18-35.

After praising John as the greatest of the prophets and after the people rejoiced because they had been baptized by him, Luke records Jesus as saying, "For John the Baptist has come eating no bread and drinking no wine; and you say, 'He has a demon.' The

Son of man has come eating and drinking; and you say, 'Behold, a glutton and a drunkard, a friend of tax collectors and sinners!' " Verses 33, 34.

Within Luke's account of the anointing of Jesus, we again see the motif of salvation along side the motif of rejection. After telling Simon the parable of the two debtors who were forgiven by their creditor, Jesus asked, "Now which of them will love him more?" Luke 7:42. Simon, of course, judged correctly, when he responded, "The one, I suppose, to whom he forgave more." Verse 43. Then, referring to the woman that Simon had called a sinner, Jesus said, "Therefore I tell you, her sins, which are many, are forgiven, for she loved much; but he who is forgiven little, loves little." Verse 47. Then Jesus said to the woman, "Your sins are forgiven. . . . Your faith has saved you; go in peace." Verses 48-50

There is no question that this passage, rewritten by Luke (thus not to be found in Matthew and Mark), also deals with the theme of salvation. But what is thrilling about Jesus' statement to the woman is the assurance of salvation that He gave to her. Twice Jesus stated that her sins had already been forgiven, and then He added that she stood in a saved relationship to Him.

This assurance is conveyed by the tense of the verbs used by Jesus. The three verbs used here are in the perfect tense. This tense communicates the fact that an action has been completed in the past and that the result of the action continues on at the time a person speaks or writes about it. Therefore, when Jesus told Simon that her sins "had been forgiven" (apheōntai, verse 47) and assured the woman that her sins "had been forgiven" (apheōntai, verse 48), He was indicating that her past sins had been wiped away and that she now stood in a forgiven relationship to Him. When Jesus told the woman that her faith "had saved" her (sesōken, verse 50), He indicated that at the moment when her sins had been forgiven, she had entered into a saved relationship to Him and was still in that relationship when Simon thought so disparagingly of her. Simon was completely out of order to regard this woman in the way he did.

Luke alone, among the synoptic writers, recorded in this way the fact that Jesus gave to people the assurance that they were saved. We have a second occurrence when Jesus spoke to the Samaritan leper who returned, and falling upon his face at Jesus' feet, thanked Jesus for healing him. Luke 17:11-19. Jesus said, " 'Were not ten cleansed? Where are the nine? Was no one found to return and give praise to God except this foreigner?' And he said to him, 'Rise and go your way; your faith has made you well [sesōken].' " Verses 17-19.

Unfortunately, the translators of the RSV have missed the whole point of Jesus' words. The Greek word "to save" (sōdzō) is used for healing (make whole, make well, etc.), because the one who is healed is saved from the disease with which he was afflicted. But is this the case here? All ten lepers were healed, only one returned to render thanks. He alone made a cognative transfer from physical leprosy to the spiritual leprosy of sin. When the cleansed leper approached Jesus the second time, it was not to find physical cleansing, but spiritual cleansing.

At the time of the first meeting between Jesus and this man, Jesus extended physical cleansing. At the second meeting, Jesus extended spiritual cleansing, "Your faith has saved [sesōken] you." Luke alone recorded the experience of this Samaritan leper. That he wished his readers to see this man as entering a saved relationship with Jesus seems clear when we consider what immediately follows. Again, it is something that Luke alone records. "Being asked by the Pharisees when the kingdom of God was coming, he answered them, 'The kingdom of God is not coming with signs to be observed; nor will they say, "Lo, here it is!" or "There!" for behold the kingdom of God is in the midst of you.' " Verses 20, 21.

Again, the translators of the RSV miss Jesus' point by saying the "kingdom of God is in the midst of you." They also miss the relationship between the Samaritan leper and the answer given to the Pharisees' question. Jesus' answer is better translated, "the kingdom of God is within you."There are two problems that must be solved before we can see the true import of Jesus' words to the Samaritan. First, can it be shown that "within you" is the correct translation and not "in the midst of you," as the RSV presents the text? Second, what is the relationship between "within you" and Jesus' statement "your faith has saved you"?

We will clear up the confusion in Jesus' answer to the question posed by the Pharisees first. The text tells us that the kingdom of God is *entos* you. Should this be understood as "in the midst of" or as "within"? If Luke wanted to say that the kingdom was "in the midst of" or "among" Jesus' hearers, it would seem that he would have used the construction that he has used on seventeen occasions in his Gospel to express this concept (i.e., the preposition *en* with the locative case). However, in verse 21, Luke used a word that appears on only one other occasion, *entos*. This word may be translated "within" or "among." However, because Luke used *en* along with the locative case seventeen times to express the concept "among" or "in the midst of," it would seem that he does not wish us to understand *entos* this way in verse 21.

The only other time *entos* appears in the New Testament is in Matthew 23:26, and the RSV translates this verse as follows: "You blind Pharisee! first cleanse the inside [*entos*] of the cup and of the plate, that the outside also may be clean." It is clear that *entos* means "within" or "inside" in this verse. Because Luke used another way to express the idea of "among" or "in the midst of," as do the other synoptic writers, *entos* should be translated "within" in Luke 17:21.

Therefore, Jesus tells the Pharisees who questioned Him about the coming of the kingdom that the kingdom resides within the hearts of men. What does this truth have to do with the Samaritan leper? Because Luke alone records the cleansing of the ten lepers and the answer to the question of the Pharisees about the kingdom, and because he places them side by side, we can see the experience of the Samaritan leper as an example of the truth Jesus taught about the kingdom. The statement of Jesus to the leper, "Your faith has saved [*sesōken*] you" (not "made you well"), is to be understood in conjunction with Jesus' answer to the Pharisees, "the kingdom of God is within you" (not "in the midst of you"). The Samaritan leper is an example of one who found the kingdom of God. It was established within his heart. Therefore, Jesus could say to him, "Your faith has saved you."

The experience of the leper is identical to that of the woman who anointed Jesus' feet. Both stood in a saved relationship with Jesus. Only Luke presents this assurance of salvation by reporting the experience of these two people. He is, no doubt, reflecting what he learned from the apostle Paul. For Paul presented the same assurance in his teaching, "For by grace you have been saved through faith." Ephesians 2:8.

One of the most outstanding examples of assurance of salvation is found in Jesus' words to the repentant criminal on the cross. Luke 23:39-43. The story of the repentant criminal who rebuked his fellow criminal for his blasphemy in railing against Jesus (verses 39-41) adds to the motif of Jesus' innocence, which Luke constructs in his passion narrative, "this man has done nothing wrong." Verse 41. Then, turning to Jesus, the criminal said, "Jesus, remember me when you come into your kingdom." Verse 42. Jesus responded with the assurance of salvation, "Truly I say to you today, you will be with me in Paradise." Verse 43. (Note, the author has relocated the controversial comma in the RSV.)

The assurance of salvation given to this man fits into the overall interest of Luke in this motif. Again, Matthew and Mark do not record this event. The experience of this man stands alongside that of the woman who anointed Jesus' feet and the Samaritan leper. All three stood in a saved relationship with Jesus, and Jesus gave to all three the assurance that this was so.

Luke adds to the motif of salvation by reporting additional parables that were given by Jesus. The parable of the lost sheep is universally recognized as a parable of salvation. Matthew records it (18:12-14), as well as Luke (15:3-7). It is not present in Mark. When you compare the context of this parable in Matthew with that of Luke, you discover that Luke adds two additional parables that Matthew does not have—the parable of the lost coin (verses 8-10) and the parable of the prodigal son (verses 11-32). Both of these parables have the same theme as the lost sheep—that which has been lost is found. So again, we see Luke, by the use of these two parables, extending the emphasis on salvation beyond that which is found in Matthew and Mark.

We will look at one more example in Luke. Only Luke tells us about Zacchaeus. Luke 19:1-10. The story of this little man is another example of Luke's interest in how the despised and the cast-offs of society responded to Jesus and how Jesus took great interest in them. The story of Zacchaeus ends with a salvation statement by Jesus, "Today salvation has come to this house." Verse 9.

Again we have seen one of the synoptic writers working as an author and theologian. All three are interested in the salvation that God brings to the human race through His Son, but they present this truth in their own individual ways. However, Luke shows a special interest in this subjet and demonstrates his interest by adding a great deal of material to his Gospel that comes to bear on this subject, material that is not found in Matthew and Mark. This added material is dispersed throughout his Gospel, and the reader can trace this theme from beginning to end. This is further evidence of Luke working as a creative author under the Lucan model of inspiration.

References

1. George E. Rice, *Christ in Collision* (Mountain View, Calif.: Paicfic Press Publishing Association, 1982), pp. 111-122.

2. *Ibid.*, pp. 100-110.

3. William F. Arndt, *The Gospel According to St. Luke* (St. Louis: Concordia Publishing House, 1956), p. 220.

Conclusion

The thought of a second model of inspiration may surprise many people. But for decades Adventist writers have sensed the fact that the prophetic model cannot adequately explain everything that we see in Scripture. That inspired writers "borrowed" or "copied" from various sources, biblical and nonbiblical, has been recognzied for years. But this phenomenon has always been addressed under the umbrella of the prophetic model, and it has always been subordinated to the supernatural—dreams and visions.

Without question, writers on the topic of inspiration would much rather explore and expound the supernatural. The unexciting, mundane work of research, which resulted in "copying" and "borrowing" from sources, is dealt with in a secondary way. Thus the impression is given that this element in the experience we call inspiration is unimportant, and at times a nuisance—something to be noted briefly in order to account for some strange phenomenon in Scripture, and then back to the supernatural—the real business of inspiration.

Because the prohetic model has been stressed and the second model has been ignored, a misunderstanding of inspiration is widespread. This misunderstanding has fostered many and various problems, the latest of which is the idea that a person who has been given the gift of prophecy negates this gift and disqualifies himself/herself as a spokesperson for God if in his or her research he or she "borrows" or "copies" from other writers. Such books as Daniel, Isaiah, Jeremiah, Ezekiel, and others prove this notion to be false, for these men whom Bible-believing Christians agree had the gift of prohecy, also demonstrate that portions of their books were written under the Lucan model of inspiration. On the other hand, the synoptic Gospels and other books show that entire books can be written under the Lucan model and then take their rightful place in the canon of Scripture as authoritative and inspired.

The charge that Ellen White cannot fill the role of a spokesperson for God or that she could not possibly have received the gift of prophecy because she "borrowed" is rooted in a misunderstanding of inspiration. Once the Lucan model is established and accepted, this model can then be allowed to explain the work of Ellen White.

This book was written with the aim of bringing the second model of inspiration to the forefront. Placing this second model alongside the prophetic model in the thinking of those who are concerned with the issues of inspiration provides a balanced understanding of and approach to these issues.